FLORENCE TOU

Explore the timeless charm of Florence and the rolling hills of Tuscany with insider tips, hidden gems, and unforgettable cultural experiences. Your essential companion for art, food, history, and adventure in the heart of Italy.

SERENA VELLORI

Copyright © Serena Vellori, 2025.

Exclusive rights to reproduce, distribute, and create derivative works of Florence travel guide, while retaining ownership and moral rights. The agreement includes royalties, anti-piracy measures, and the use of digital rights management (DRM). The Author reserves the right to terminate the agreement.

Disclaimer

The information contained in this book is for educational and informational purposes only. While every effort has been made to ensure accuracy, the author and publisher assume no responsibility for any errors or omissions, nor for any consequences arising from the use of the information herein. The views expressed in this book are those of the author and do not necessarily reflect the opinions of any affiliated institutions, organizations, or entities.

Table of Contents

FLORENCE TRAVEL GUIDE TOUR 2025 1

   Explore the timeless charm of Florence and the rolling hills of Tuscany with insider tips, hidden gems, and unforgettable cultural experiences. Your essential companion for art, food, history, and adventure in the heart of Italy. 1

Chapter 1 10

A Poetic Arrival in Florence 10

   First Impressions: Stone, Scent, and Renaissance Charm 10

   Understanding Florence's Layout: Historic Center and Neighborhoods 12

   Adjusting to the Pace: Jet Lag, Italian Time, and Local Rhythm 14

Chapter 2 17

A Walk Through the Renaissance 17

   Exploring Piazza del Duomo and the Cathedral of Santa Maria del Fiore 17

   Palazzo Vecchio, Piazza della Signoria, and Political Florence 19

   Ponte Vecchio and the Arno River's Historic Soul 21

Chapter 3 24

- The Art That Changed the World 24
  - Uffizi Gallery: Botticelli, Caravaggio, and Beyond 24
  - Accademia Gallery: Michelangelo's David and Artistic Mastery 26
  - Small Museums and Frescoed Chapels Off the Beaten Path 29
- Chapter 4 31
- Churches and Sacred Beauty 31
  - Florence's Spiritual Heart: Duomo, Santa Croce, and Santa Maria Novella 31
  - San Miniato al Monte: Florence from Above, with Soul 33
  - Art in Churches: Giotto, Masaccio, Brunelleschi's Legacy 35
- Chapter 5 37
- Florence From Above 37
  - Climbing the Duomo and Giotto's Bell Tower 37
  - Sunset at Piazzale Michelangelo 39
  - Rooftop Bars and Terraces with Unforgettable Views 40
- Chapter 6 44
- Tuscan Flavors and Where to Find Them 44

Must-Try Florentine Dishes: Bistecca, Pappa al Pomodoro, Lampredotto 44

Trattorias, Osterias, and Authentic Dining Spots 46

Mercato Centrale and Sant'Ambrogio Market Adventures 49

Chapter 7 52

Aperitivo Culture and Cafés of the City 52

How to Do Aperitivo Like a Local: Times, Places, Etiquette 52

Best Cafés for People-Watching and Espresso Moments 54

Iconic Bars: Caffè Gilli, Rivoire, Ditta Artigianale 56

Chapter 8 60

Bars, Clubs, and Florence After Dark 60

Where to Dance: Otel, Tenax, YAB, and Late-Night Rhythm 60

Wine Bars and Speakeasies for Slow Evenings 61

LGBTQ+-Friendly Nightlife and Inclusive Spaces 63

Chapter 9 66

Shopping and Artisan Streets 66

Leather Markets, Goldsmiths, and Florentine Craftsmanship 66

Oltrarno's Artisans: Paper, Perfume, Frames, and Fine Art 68

Where to Buy Souvenirs with Heart (and How to Avoid Tourist Traps) 70

Chapter 10 73

Hidden Florence – Secrets and Silence 73

Quiet Cloisters, Secret Gardens, and Whispering Fountains 73

Abandoned Towers and Hidden Alleys 75

Convents, Artisan Courtyards, and Places of Stillness 76

Chapter 11 79

Romantic Florence for Two 79

Best Spots for Couples: Gardens, Rooftops, and Strolls 79

Proposal and Honeymoon Inspiration in Historic Settings 81

Private Dinners, Art Dates, and Bespoke Couple Activities 82

Chapter 12 85

Florence for Families and Kids 85

Kid-Friendly Museums and Creative Workshops 85

Parks, Puppet Shows, and Space to Roam 87

Family Restaurants and Gelato Stops Children Will Love 89

Chapter 13 92

Faith, Religion, and Cultural Rituals 92

The Catholic Heartbeat: Daily Rituals, Bells, and Mass 92

Patron Saint Festivals and Religious Processions 94

Religion in Everyday Life: Icons, Gestures, and Respect 97

Chapter 14 100

Festivals, Holidays, and Local Celebrations 100

Scoppio del Carro (Explosion of the Cart) and Easter Traditions 100

Calcio Storico: Florence's Historical Sport with Passion 102

Pitti Uomo, Christmas Lights, and Summertime Street Festivals 104

Chapter 15 107

Florence by Season 107

Spring: Wisteria Blooms, Garden Walks, and Easter Magic 107

Summer: Sun-Soaked Piazzas, Longer Days, and Evening Life 108

Autumn and Winter: Truffle Season, Holiday Markets, and Quiet Beauty 110

Chapter 16 112

Day Trips and Tuscan Escapes 112

Siena, Pisa, and the Chianti Wine Region 112

Lucca and Fiesole: Hilltowns with Heart 114

Tips for Taking Trains, Buses, or Car Rentals from Florence 116

Chapter 17 119

Practical Travel Tips and Street Smarts 119

How to Navigate Florence: Walking, Taxis, Scooters, Buses 119

Common Tourist Mistakes and How to Avoid Them 121

Blending In: Greetings, Style, Language, and Local Dos & Don'ts 123

Chapter 18 125

Emergency Numbers and Useful Contacts 125

Emergency Services: Police (112), Ambulance (118), Fire (115) 125

24-Hour Pharmacies, Hospitals, and Late-Night Help 127

Lost Items, Embassy Contacts, SIM Cards, and Tourist Information Centers 129

Chapter 1
A Poetic Arrival in Florence

First Impressions: Stone, Scent, and Renaissance Charm

The first time I stepped onto the stone-paved streets of Florence, it felt like I had slipped into a painting—an oil canvas kissed by sunlight, brushed with centuries of genius and soul. I had read about the city countless times, studied its Renaissance legacy, admired photos of its domes and statues, yet nothing prepared me for the sheer beauty of *being here*. Florence doesn't simply welcome you—it unveils itself slowly, like a secret whispered in Italian.

It was early afternoon when I arrived at Santa Maria Novella train station. I stepped out with my suitcase rattling over uneven cobblestones, the sound almost musical against the backdrop of Italian voices, bells tolling faintly in the distance, and the rhythmic hum of mopeds weaving through the streets. The air was thick with warmth and nostalgia. There was something intoxicating in it—a mix of espresso, warm stone, and the distant sweetness of blooming jasmine. Everything smelled old and alive at the same time.

As I turned the corner from the station and caught my first glimpse of the Duomo—Santa Maria del Fiore—I stopped in my tracks. The cathedral rose like a dream in marble and terracotta, its massive red dome soaring into the sky, flanked by Giotto's Bell Tower. The white and green patterns on its façade shimmered in the sunlight like lace carved in stone. I stood there, suitcase forgotten, eyes wide, heart full. It was my first real moment of *awe* in Florence, and it would not be my last.

The streets felt like a labyrinth of stories. On Via dei Calzaiuoli, I wandered past leather shops that smelled like craftsmanship, past cafes filled with clinking cups and contented chatter. Artists painted on sidewalks. Children played with gelato-stained fingers. Everything felt cinematic, like every frame was composed by a master director who understood the weight of beauty.

There's a sacred stillness in Florence even amid the bustle. The city moves, but never rushes. Its pace invites you to slow down, breathe deeply, and look closer. I quickly realized this wasn't a place for checklist tourism. It was a place for wandering, pausing, and *feeling*. Florence didn't need to impress me. It simply *was*—and that was enough.

Understanding Florence's Layout: Historic Center and Neighborhoods

It took me a couple of days to truly grasp the layout of Florence. At first, everything felt like a maze of narrow streets and centuries-old buildings that all looked charmingly similar. But Florence, like a well-structured novel, has chapters. And once you understand its narrative, the story becomes easier to follow.

At the center of it all is the **Centro Storico**, the historic heart of the city. This is where Florence began, where its soul resides. Bordered roughly by the Arno River to the south and by viali di circonvallazione (the wide 19th-century boulevards), the center is walkable, intimate, and brimming with life. Every step seems to lead to another piazza, another church, another story. Within just a few minutes' walk, you can reach the Duomo, the Uffizi Gallery, Palazzo Vecchio, and Ponte Vecchio. It's astonishing how much world-changing beauty is packed into such a compact area.

To the **south of the Arno**, across the famous **Ponte Vecchio**, lies **Oltrarno**—literally "the other side of the Arno." This neighborhood quickly became my favorite. It's quieter, more local, less polished. It feels like Florence exhaling. This is where you find artisan workshops, humble trattorias, and sun-drenched piazzas like Santo Spirito, where locals sip Spritz in the evening and artists sell their paintings on blankets.

Further north, near the **Mercato Centrale** and **San Lorenzo**, I discovered a more chaotic, colorful Florence—where students from the University of Florence mingle with market vendors, where street food meets high fashion. The Medici Chapels rise proudly here, nestled among leather stalls and souvenir shops.

And then there's **Santa Croce**, to the east—a neighborhood that felt like a historical treasure chest. This is where Michelangelo and Galileo rest. The basilica is grand, but the streets around it are simple and real. I spent one of my favorite evenings sitting on the church steps, listening to a cellist play under the twilight sky, the crowd hushed and spellbound.

An illustrated map of Florence with a personal touch—highlighting major neighborhoods like Centro Storico, Oltrarno, San Lorenzo,

Florence may look small on a map, but each neighborhood offers its own emotion. The city unfolds slowly, street by street, like a mosaic. And once you learn its rhythm, you stop trying to control the journey and start letting Florence lead.

Adjusting to the Pace: Jet Lag, Italian Time, and Local Rhythm

The first few days in Florence, I fought time. I tried to wake early, squeeze in museums, check off every site I'd read about. But Florence isn't made for that. My jet-lagged brain kept buzzing, but the city had other ideas. It wanted me to sit longer over my cappuccino, to watch the old men play cards in Piazza della Repubblica, to *listen* to the bells instead of chasing them.

On my third morning, I surrendered.

I woke naturally, late. I strolled to a corner café and ordered a **cappuccino e cornetto con crema**—no to-go cup, no rush. I sat in the sun. I watched pigeons court each other. I saw lovers walk hand-in-hand, not speaking, just *being*. That's when I understood Italian time. It's not about efficiency—it's about presence. Italians aren't lazy. They're **attuned**. They know that life is richer when savored.

Florence, in particular, teaches you this. It's a city that begs for long meals, longer walks, and moments of stillness. I stopped feeling guilty for not "doing enough." Instead, I started *feeling* enough.

I learned that:

- **Museums open late** in the morning—plan brunch first.
- **Shops close mid-day** (often from 1–3 p.m.)—use this time to nap or read by the Arno.
- **Dinner starts after 7:30 p.m.**, and aperitivo begins around 6 p.m.—don't rush either.

Evenings became my favorite. Florence glows golden after 6 p.m. The streets soften. Locals emerge. The tourists thin out. One evening, I sat on the **Arno bridge at golden hour**, listening to street musicians, eating gelato from **La Carraia**, and watching the light paint the water in amber and rose. It was the closest thing to prayer I've ever experienced.

In adjusting to Florence, I adjusted to myself. I allowed stillness. I allowed slowness. And in that slowness, I discovered a deeper kind of joy—the joy of presence.

Florence doesn't just give you art and architecture. It gives you *permission*. Permission to wander. To feel. To rest. To marvel. To fall in love with the old and the timeless, with the streets and yourself. My arrival in Florence wasn't marked by fireworks or fanfare. It was marked by quiet wonder. And in that quiet, something awakened in me—something that hadn't stirred in years.

The city doesn't demand your attention. It *deserves* it. And the longer you stay, the more you understand that every stone has a story, every café a memory waiting to be made. So take it slow. Breathe deeply. Let Florence unfold. Because once it does, it will never leave you.

Chapter 2
A Walk Through the Renaissance

Exploring Piazza del Duomo and the Cathedral of Santa Maria del Fiore

The first time I stepped into **Piazza del Duomo**, I felt tiny—and not in a way that made me feel small, but in a way that made me feel humbled by grandeur. Everything around me towered and shimmered. The *Cathedral of Santa Maria del Fiore* stood like a Renaissance colossus, a masterpiece of marble and mystery. Its dome, Brunelleschi's impossible feat, looked like it had been dropped from the sky by the gods. How could something this massive, this intricate, this *perfect*, have been built so long ago?

I stood in silence for a long time, watching tourists tilt their heads, photographers adjust their lenses, and artists sketch quietly in corners. I was one of them—trying to take it all in. The scent of warm stone and espresso filled the air. Horse-drawn carriages passed lazily by. Children danced in the fountain's mist. The square wasn't just alive—it was *singing*.

The Duomo isn't just an architectural marvel. It's the *beating heart* of Florence. For centuries, it's anchored the city through war, plague, and peace. Inside, the grandeur continues—Vasari's fresco of the Last

Judgment in the dome, the vast silence of the nave, the tomb of Filippo Brunelleschi himself. But it was the dome climb that changed me.

Climbing up the tight staircase—463 steps—I felt like I was crawling through the arteries of Florence's soul. At every turn, frescoes loomed above me. As I neared the top, the light shifted. And then, suddenly, I emerged outside—and the entire city was below me. Terracotta rooftops, church spires, olive-green hills in the distance. I could see **everything**. Florence wasn't just a city. It was a Renaissance made stone and sky.

A panoramic shot with Giotto's Bell Tower

Next to the Duomo, **Giotto's Bell Tower** rises with its pink, white, and green marble panels catching the light. And behind the cathedral, the **Baptistery of San**

Giovanni dazzles with its golden mosaics and the famed **Gates of Paradise** by Ghiberti. These buildings form a holy trinity of art and devotion, where every inch tells a story.

Walking through this square at different times of day became a ritual for me. At sunrise, it was quiet, the marble glowing softly. At midday, alive and humming. At night, lit in amber and silver, it felt eternal. I often sat on the steps outside, watching the city breathe. Florence, I realized, doesn't just preserve history—it invites you to *inhabit* it.

Palazzo Vecchio, Piazza della Signoria, and Political Florence

From the Duomo, I wandered south—only five minutes on foot, yet it felt like entering another era entirely. **Piazza della Signoria** opened before me like a grand Renaissance stage. Every building, every statue, every flag told a story of power, revolution, and human ambition. I was walking through Florence's **political heart**, and I could *feel* it.

Dominating the square is the **Palazzo Vecchio**, a fortress-like town hall with its medieval tower stabbing the sky. I remember the first time I stood beneath it. Its size was impressive, but it was the weight of its history that floored me. This is where Machiavelli once walked. Where the Medici family ruled with cunning and grace. Where public executions and civic speeches shaped the course of European history.

I entered the palazzo with reverence. Inside, the **Salone dei Cinquecento** stunned me into silence. The ceiling stretched above like a frescoed tapestry. Vasari's paintings swirled in battle scenes, glory, and myth. Every corridor whispered secrets of diplomacy and drama. I stood in the room where Cosimo I plotted, where art and politics collided in ways still felt today.

Outside, the square is a sculpture garden under the open sky. The **Loggia dei Lanzi**, with its stone arches, houses some of the most emotionally charged works I've ever seen: Cellini's *Perseus with the Head of Medusa*, Giambologna's *Rape of the Sabine Women*, and ancient Roman lions that still stand watch.

And then, of course, there is **David**—or rather, **a replica** of Michelangelo's masterpiece standing where the original once did. Even though the real David is now housed safely in the Accademia Gallery, this copy still commands attention. His stance, his stare, his defiance—it's all there, reminding every visitor that Florence once stood as a *David* against the Goliaths of

Europe.

A twilight shot of Piazza della Signoria—warm lighting on the Palazzo Vecchio

I came back to this square again and again. Once, I caught a street violinist playing Vivaldi at sunset. Another time, it was nearly empty after a summer rain, the flagstones glistening like glass. Each visit felt new, as if the spirits of the Renaissance were always stirring something fresh in the air.

Ponte Vecchio and the Arno River's Historic Soul

A few steps west, past more piazzas and shuttered windows, I found myself standing at the **Ponte Vecchio**—Florence's oldest and most iconic bridge. It was evening, and the light turned the Arno River into liquid gold. I'd seen this view in books and paintings, but nothing compares to standing there, leaning on the railing, watching the sun dissolve behind the Tuscan hills.

Built in 1345, the bridge is a story in itself. Once the domain of butchers and fishmongers, it now houses glittering **gold shops**, jewelers, and artisan boutiques. As I walked across, I peered into glass windows filled with necklaces and rings sparkling like captured starlight. The wooden shutters, painted in faded greens and ochres, gave the bridge the feel of a suspended village.

Above the shops runs the **Vasari Corridor**, a secret elevated passageway built for the Medici to move safely between Palazzo Vecchio and Palazzo Pitti. As I stood on the bridge, I imagined them walking above me—plotting alliances, escaping enemies, observing the city they ruled without being seen.

The **Arno River** itself is the soul of Florence. It has flooded and shaped the city, carried trade and tragedy, inspired poets and painters. Sitting on the stone steps of the **Lungarno**, I felt peace like nowhere else in the city. The water moved slow and deep, reflecting the old bridges and the fading sky.

At night, the riverbanks shimmer. Couples stroll. Cyclists pass quietly. Lamps cast golden circles on the cobblestones. I'd sometimes sit there with gelato in one hand and my journal in the other, writing whatever came to mind. Often, I wrote nothing—just breathed it all in.

The Ponte Vecchio is more than a bridge. It's a symbol. A spine of connection, of resilience. It has survived floods and wars, even Hitler's bombs, which destroyed every other bridge in the city during World War II. And still, it stands.

Walking through these spaces—the Duomo, Piazza della Signoria, and Ponte Vecchio—isn't just sightseeing. It's stepping into the **heartbeat of the Renaissance**. It's where power met beauty, where politics met poetry, where stone met soul.

Each street I walked in Florence felt like a brushstroke on a canvas already thick with meaning. And as I walked, I wasn't just learning history—I was *becoming part of it*. The Renaissance isn't trapped in museums. It breathes through Florence. Through the arches. Through the bells. Through every step echoing on marble.

Chapter 3
The Art That Changed the World
Uffizi Gallery: Botticelli, Caravaggio, and Beyond
The morning I visited the **Uffizi Gallery**, I woke up early—too early for a city that thrives on slow espresso and gentle beginnings. The streets were still wet from overnight rain, and the air carried a chill that made every marble step feel alive beneath my boots. I wasn't rushing. I was preparing myself. Because you don't just *visit* the Uffizi. You surrender to it.

Located between Piazza della Signoria and the Arno, the Uffizi's courtyard alone is like a passage through time. I walked slowly beneath the stone colonnades, flanked by statues of Galileo, Dante, and Michelangelo, as if entering a temple. And in many ways, I was. **A temple of art. A cathedral of human imagination.**

I entered just after it opened, hoping to beat the crowd. I climbed the long staircase, the light filtering through ancient windows. The moment I stepped into the first gallery, time lost meaning. The walls whispered. The paintings watched.

There's a hush that falls over you when you stand in front of **Botticelli's "Birth of Venus."** It's not just the beauty—it's the boldness. That hair flowing like a river of gold. That gaze—detached, divine. And the realization that this was painted over five centuries ago. I stood there for nearly twenty minutes, the crowd around me shifting and breathing, but I didn't move. In that moment, I felt as if I, too, had been born from a shell on the shore of an ancient sea.

And then came **Caravaggio**. If Botticelli was the dream, Caravaggio was the storm. His *Medusa*—a severed head staring in agony, painted on a ceremonial shield—stopped me cold. So much motion in a frozen scream. His realism is terrifying, magnetic. Where Botticelli invited wonder, Caravaggio confronted truth.

The Uffizi flows like a novel, room by room. Giotto, Lippi, Da Vinci, Raphael, Titian—every name is a chapter in the story of humanity finding its voice. The ceilings are painted. The corridors echo with reverence. And just when you think you've seen it all, you reach the **Vasari Corridor's exit view**, where the Arno glitters through the glass and the rooftops of Florence glow like terracotta poetry.

An interior shot of the Uffizi's Botticelli room—"Birth of Venus" taking center stage.

I left the Uffizi exhausted and elated. The kind of tired that comes from deep feeling, not just walking. Florence didn't just show me art that day—it showed me the soul of a civilization that once dared to believe beauty could *save us all*.

Accademia Gallery: Michelangelo's David and Artistic Mastery

The next morning, I made my pilgrimage to see **David**.

The **Galleria dell'Accademia** is smaller, less imposing than the Uffizi, tucked into a side street near Piazza San Marco. From the outside, you wouldn't suspect that it holds one of the most **awe-inspiring works of art in history**. But once inside, the space builds to a single crescendo.

I passed through rooms of altarpieces, musical instruments, unfinished sculptures. And then, I turned the corner—and there he was.

David.

Michelangelo's David doesn't merely stand. He **rises**. Thirteen feet of marble transformed into flesh and fury, resolve and grace. His muscles are tense, but his face is calm. He isn't fighting. He's *becoming*. And in that, I saw something deeply human.

There's a stillness in the gallery that feels sacred. People whisper, as though standing in a chapel. I circled the statue, slowly. From the sinew of his neck to the veins in his hand, every detail speaks of devotion, of the human body seen not as sin, but as glory.

What struck me even more were the **Prisoners**—Michelangelo's unfinished sculptures that line the corridor before you reach David. Figures caught inside blocks of marble, writhing, struggling to break free. He didn't finish them, yet they tell a story just as powerful.

The idea that art isn't about perfection, but about **liberation**.

A dramatic shot of Michelangelo's David under the gallery's oculus light—soft shadows falling on his chest and limbs.

In seeing David, I didn't just admire a masterpiece. I understood something about courage. About standing naked before the world with nothing but your faith and your stones. David is not just art. He's a reminder that **greatness often begins with stillness, vulnerability, and the willingness to face giants.**

Small Museums and Frescoed Chapels Off the Beaten Path

But it wasn't just the Uffizi or the Accademia that moved me. Some of the deepest, most intimate experiences I had with art happened in places most tourists never find.

One rainy afternoon, I wandered into **Museo di San Marco**, once a Dominican monastery. Inside, I found silence—and the world of **Fra Angelico**. Each monk's cell was painted with a fresco—small, quiet scenes of Christ, rendered not for crowds but for contemplation. I stepped into one room and found "The Annunciation." Mary, blue-robed and wide-eyed, receives her destiny in a shaft of light. There were no crowds. Just me. And the sound of the rain outside. It felt like the painting was *waiting for me*.

Then there was **Cappella Brancacci**, hidden within the Church of Santa Maria del Carmine in the Oltrarno. Here, **Masaccio's frescoes** opened my eyes to the birth of Renaissance realism. The *Expulsion from the Garden of Eden*—Adam's face twisted in grief, Eve covering herself in shame—felt raw and immediate. It was the first time I saw human emotion captured like this in paint. It was 600 years old. It might as well have been yesterday.

And perhaps the most unexpected moment happened at **Museo Horne**, a small house-museum filled with quiet treasures. There was no crowd, no noise. Just a few rooms, a few oil paintings, and the hushed intimacy of a collector's love letter to the Renaissance. I sat in a carved wooden chair and stared at a panel by Filippino Lippi for twenty minutes. Not because it was famous. But because it *spoke to me*.

These smaller spaces didn't shout for attention. They *whispered*. And in those whispers, I heard the echoes of devotion, of craft, of art made not for galleries, but for **souls**.

Florence changed the world through art—not by force, but by **showing us what was possible**. That we could shape marble into gods. That we could paint light into existence. That beauty could challenge power, heal grief, and stir joy.

In Florence, art is not on display. It is *alive*. It watches you back. It teaches you not just to look—but to see. And when you leave, you are not the same.

Chapter 4
Churches and Sacred Beauty

Florence's Spiritual Heart: Duomo, Santa Croce, and Santa Maria Novella

I thought I had seen beauty before I came to Florence—but I hadn't seen **sacred beauty**. Not the kind that hums in the air, that presses gently on your chest, that makes your breath slow just so your soul can catch up. Florence doesn't just house churches. It *is* a church. A cathedral of history, devotion, and light—where every stone was placed not just for worship, but for wonder.

Though I had already marveled at the **Duomo** from the outside, stepping back inside after days of wandering through Florence's neighborhoods felt different. As if I'd grown quiet enough inside myself to finally hear what it was trying to say.

Inside, it's unexpectedly spare—cool, vast, almost austere. But above, the **dome by Brunelleschi**, frescoed by Vasari and Zuccari, bursts with color and movement. The Last Judgment spirals overhead: angels, demons, saints, and sinners—chaos painted onto symmetry. I sat down on a wooden pew and stared up for what felt like hours. I didn't pray. I just listened.

A few blocks east, I found **Santa Croce**—grand and weathered, with a wide piazza that catches the morning sun. It's not just a church—it's **Florence's pantheon**, holding the tombs of Galileo, Machiavelli, Michelangelo. I walked along the nave, passing sculpted monuments that looked like dreams carved in stone. But it was Michelangelo's tomb that stilled me. Three figures—representing Painting, Sculpture, and Architecture—mourned his passing. I placed my hand over my heart and whispered, *Grazie*.

And then there was **Santa Maria Novella**, the first church I ever entered in Florence, just steps from the train station—and yet, few travelers seem to stop inside. Their loss. The church is magnificent. A swirl of Gothic and early Renaissance design, filled with stained glass and harmony. It holds treasures: Masaccio's Holy Trinity, Giotto's crucifix, fresco cycles that pull you into biblical stories like portals. The cloisters outside are peaceful, ringed with cypress trees and quiet benches.

Each of these churches is a pillar of Florence's identity. More than landmarks, they are **living spaces** where art and soul meet, where tourists become pilgrims without even realizing it.

San Miniato al Monte: Florence from Above, with Soul

I didn't expect **San Miniato al Monte** to move me the way it did. It's not as famous as the Duomo. It's not as central as Santa Croce. You have to *climb* to get there—up the steps behind Piazzale Michelangelo, through quiet gardens and the scent of rosemary. But the climb is worth it. In every way.

The church sits like a crown above the city. When I reached the top, Florence opened up before me—**an ocean of rooftops**, the Arno snaking through its heart, the dome of the Duomo rising like a compass needle pointing to the heavens. I stood there, breathless, both from the climb and the view. It felt like Florence was **offering itself to me**, completely.

The facade of San Miniato is a mosaic of green and white marble, glowing in the late afternoon sun. Inside, the church is dim, ancient, and intimate. Frescoes whisper from the walls. The floor, a geometric puzzle of inlaid marble. The crypt, shrouded in candlelight, is still tended by monks who chant Vespers most evenings. I was lucky enough to be there as the singing began—deep, resonant voices rising through the ancient stone.

The stillness in that moment felt sacred. I was not alone, but the silence between us all was full of meaning.

Outside, the world buzzed. But in here, in this space of song and stone, **time stopped**.

A golden-hour view from the steps of San Miniato al Monte—overlooking Florence below, with the Duomo in the distance.

I sat outside the church afterward, watching swallows dart through the sky. I had come up for a view—and found a piece of myself instead. San Miniato isn't just Florence from above. It's Florence *with soul*. A city wrapped in silence, sunlight, and song.

Art in Churches: Giotto, Masaccio, Brunelleschi's Legacy

One of the most incredible things about Florence is that **you don't have to go to a museum to see world-changing art**. It's in the churches. Hanging over altars. Hidden behind columns. Painted into chapels that still smell of incense and candle wax.

I remember the first time I saw **Giotto's crucifix** hanging in Santa Maria Novella. Christ's body was elongated and heavy, not idealized but human. You could see the pain in His face. It wasn't just a painting. It was a **revolution**. Giotto pulled art from the flatness of medieval icons into something more honest, more dimensional. It changed how artists saw the world—and how they painted it.

Then came **Masaccio**, whose frescoes in the **Brancacci Chapel** are so raw, so real, they feel like cinema before cinema existed. His "Expulsion from Eden" hit me the hardest. Adam's face twisted in grief. Eve covering herself in shame. The emotion was almost unbearable. I remember looking around the chapel and seeing other visitors blinking back tears. This wasn't just art. It was **empathy on a wall**.

And then, of course, there's **Brunelleschi**—not just the man who built the dome of the Duomo, but the architect who transformed sacred space. Inside **San Lorenzo**, his proportions soothe the soul. Clean lines. Harmony. Balance. It feels modern, even now. Standing in that church, I understood how geometry could be spiritual—how space itself could lead us to wonder.

These churches don't merely display art. They *are* art. Built and painted by men who believed beauty was a path to the divine. And maybe it is. Because as I wandered from altar to altar, fresco to fresco, I didn't feel like I was learning history. I felt like I was remembering something my heart already knew.

Florence's churches are more than places of worship. They are **archives of the soul**. Each one carries the hopes, fears, talents, and prayers of a thousand years. You don't have to be religious to feel it. You just have to walk in with open eyes and an open heart.

I came to Florence searching for beauty. I found it in stone and story, in chant and chapel. And in the stillness between stained-glass shadows, I found something else too—a peace I hadn't known I was missing.

Chapter 5
Florence From Above

Climbing the Duomo and Giotto's Bell Tower

Florence isn't just a city—it's a painting come to life. But to truly see its brushstrokes, you need to **climb**. You need to rise above the narrow streets and red-tiled roofs, to a place where the Renaissance spills out in every direction like a living canvas. The day I climbed the **Duomo** and **Giotto's Bell Tower**, I didn't just conquer stairs—I ascended into *history*.

I started early. The air was crisp, the morning light slanting across the stone piazzas. I had booked my combined ticket days before, and even though my legs protested at the idea of hundreds of steps, my heart surged with excitement. Climbing the **Cupola**—Brunelleschi's masterwork—felt like stepping inside the mind of a genius.

The staircase spirals up in narrow stone corridors that twist and tighten. With every step, the sounds of the city below grow distant. Occasionally, a window opens onto the rooftops—offering a glimpse of what's to come. But the true surprise comes halfway up, when you emerge onto the interior walkway beneath the **frescoed dome**. The ceiling looms above in all its terrifying glory—**Vasari's "Last Judgment,"** swirling with angels, demons, and saints. You're close enough to see the cracks in the plaster, the brushstrokes in the wings of archangels. It's both beautiful and overwhelming, like staring directly into the heavens.

The final stretch is steep—barely room for one person at a time. And then, suddenly, I was outside, the wind pressing softly against my face. And there it was—**Florence from above**.

The city bloomed below me like a sun-drenched tapestry. **Terracotta roofs** stretched in every direction. The **Arno River** shimmered silver in the distance, crossed by Ponte Vecchio like a thread in a golden weave. I could see towers and domes, hills and vineyards, distant Tuscan farmhouses. All of it wrapped in golden light, as if the city were being held in the palm of something divine.

After descending, I walked to the nearby entrance of **Giotto's Bell Tower**. While not as dizzying as the Cupola, the **Campanile** offers its own unique reward: a side-by-side view of the Duomo dome itself. The climb—414 steps—is divided into breaks, with **arched windows** at each level letting in light and city views. Each landing felt like a breathing point, a chance to watch Florence unfold, layer by layer.

From the top, I saw the dome glowing in the afternoon sun, close enough to see its tiles and ribs. Tourists below looked like ants crawling in the piazza. The city's geometry revealed itself—**symmetry in chaos**, order in medieval design. It made me appreciate Brunelleschi's achievement even more. He didn't just build a dome. He gave Florence a **skyline**, a symbol of its soul.

Sunset at Piazzale Michelangelo

There are moments when a city stops being just a place and becomes a memory you carry forever. For me, that moment came at **sunset on Piazzale Michelangelo**.

I had heard about it before I arrived. "The best view in Florence," people said. "Go at golden hour." And so I did. I crossed the Arno via **Ponte alle Grazie**, walked past sleepy cypress trees and garden walls, then started the slow climb up **Viale Michelangiolo**. The incline was steady, the steps familiar, and the anticipation grew with every turn.

When I reached the top, the view **stole my breath**.

Florence lay stretched out below, glowing like embers beneath the setting sun. The **Duomo**, the **Palazzo Vecchio**, the bridges, the bell towers—all bathed in a warm orange-pink light. Behind them, the rolling

Tuscan hills darkened into velvet. Around me, lovers embraced. Artists painted. Travelers held their phones high and their breath low. It was silent and full all at once.

I found a spot on the edge of the stone balustrade, where someone had carved a heart into the stone. I sat there, gelato in hand (stracciatella, always), watching the sun dip slowly behind the city. And I felt it: **that Florence magic**. That moment where you're no longer a visitor. You're part of something. You belong.

As the sky shifted from gold to indigo, the city lights flickered on. One by one. Softly. Like stars waking up.

I stayed until the streetlamps buzzed to life. A street guitarist began to play "**Con te partirò**," and for a while, strangers became companions. We clapped, we swayed. Some cried. And as the final chord faded, the whole piazza applauded—not just for him, but for **Florence herself**.

Rooftop Bars and Terraces with Unforgettable Views

Florence may have been built for painters and pilgrims, but it's also a city of **cocktails and conversation**. And there's no better way to reflect on its grandeur than from above, glass in hand, surrounded by music, laughter, and a slow breeze rolling in from the Arno.

One of my favorite discoveries was the rooftop bar at **Hotel Continentale**, perched above Ponte Vecchio. It's chic, stylish, but not intimidating. The crowd is a mix of locals and travelers. I ordered a Negroni—Florence's gift to the cocktail world—and leaned against the glass railing as the sun kissed the river. The **Duomo loomed in the distance**, and the city below buzzed in miniature. The bartender lit a candle at my table. The mood shifted from day to night, like a sigh.

Later that week, I returned to the **SE·STO on Arno**, atop the Westin Excelsior. The terrace there is **pure romance**—marble tables, linen napkins, views stretching all the way to Fiesole. I ordered a plate of bruschetta and a glass of Chianti Classico. The city beneath me felt soft, distant, almost unreal. I watched as someone proposed at the next table. Applause rose with the moonlight.

But not all rooftops are formal. I also found joy at **La Terrazza at Rinascente**, right above the Piazza della Repubblica. No reservations. No dress code. Just espresso and rooftops and the carousel spinning slowly below. I sat there for hours, writing in my journal, letting Florence unfold like a song I never wanted to end.

A bar table—half-filled glass of wine, a candle flickering in a breeze, and Florence glowing below.

There's something different about Florence at rooftop level. You're above the noise, but not removed from it. You hear laughter echoing up. Church bells rolling across tiles. You watch the city soften with every passing hour. And you realize: Florence doesn't just change through the day—it changes *you*.

To see Florence from above is to understand her not just as a city, but as a **living masterpiece**. The rooftops, the rivers, the domes—they form a harmony, a perspective that lingers long after your feet return to the ground.

Whether from the heights of Brunelleschi's dome, the steps of Piazzale Michelangelo, or the rim of a wine glass on a rooftop terrace, Florence from above is a gift. A revelation. A reminder that sometimes, to truly see, you must climb.

Chapter 6
Tuscan Flavors and Where to Find Them

Must-Try Florentine Dishes: Bistecca, Pappa al Pomodoro, Lampredotto

Florence doesn't just feed you—it **seduces you**. The moment you arrive, you're wrapped in the aroma of roasted meat, simmering tomatoes, garlic sizzling in olive oil, and the soft scent of rising bread. Every street seems to promise something delicious, every doorway might lead to the best meal of your life. For me, food became a kind of pilgrimage—a way to taste the soul of Tuscany one forkful at a time.

My first real Florentine meal was a **bistecca alla fiorentina**.

I was warned. "It's big," someone told me. "It's rare. It's not just dinner—it's an *event*." I chose **Trattoria Sostanza**, a no-frills, old-school place tucked away on Via del Porcellana. The waitress didn't hand me a menu. She smiled and simply said, "Bistecca?" I nodded, nervously. Moments later, it arrived—**a massive T-bone steak**, perfectly seared on the outside, deep pink within, drizzled with local olive oil. It was almost intimidating in size and aroma.

But then I took a bite.

The crust crackled. The meat melted. It was smoky, juicy, and so flavorful I actually closed my eyes. I had never tasted anything like it. It wasn't just the cut—it was the history, the *precision*, the Florentine pride on a plate. I paired it with a glass of Chianti and some grilled vegetables, and for half an hour, I disappeared into that meal.

A few days later, craving something simpler and more comforting, I wandered into a family-run spot in Oltrarno. The owner's daughter suggested **pappa al pomodoro**, a thick tomato-and-bread soup born of Tuscan frugality. It arrived bubbling in a terracotta bowl, topped with a drizzle of olive oil and a handful of torn basil. The flavors were humble yet heavenly. Each spoonful felt like being wrapped in a warm hug from a nonna I never had.

And then there's **lampredotto**—the fourth stomach of the cow, stewed until tender and served in a crusty bun. It sounds intimidating, I know. But in Florence, **you try it**. It's tradition. I ordered mine from a street cart near Piazza della Repubblica. The man behind the counter sliced the bread, spooned in the steaming meat, topped it with salsa verde, and handed it over with a wink.

I took one bite and understood why locals queue up every day. It was earthy, rich, slightly spicy, and deeply satisfying. Street food with history. Florence on the go.

A rustic wooden table with a freshly served bistecca alla fiorentina, perfectly seared and sliced, with grilled vegetables, Chianti wine.

Florentine cuisine is simple but **soulful**. It's never about excess. It's about letting good ingredients speak—and then listening with your taste buds and your heart.

Trattorias, Osterias, and Authentic Dining Spots

If you want to eat well in Florence—and truly understand the city—you need to learn where the locals go. The real Florence isn't always in the guidebooks. It's down alleys lit by lanterns, behind wooden doors with faded signs, in rooms where the wine is poured before you even sit.

One of my favorite finds was **Trattoria Cammillo**, just south of the Arno. The menu is handwritten. The walls are lined with framed family photos. And the pasta? Life-changing. I had **tagliatelle al tartufo**—homemade pasta with truffle butter. It was velvety, rich, and utterly hypnotic. I wiped my plate clean with bread and ordered a second glass of wine just to sit there longer, soaking in the hum of Italian conversation.

On another night, I ventured to **Osteria Vini e Vecchi Sapori**, near Piazza della Signoria. It was tiny—maybe five tables. The waiter read the day's offerings aloud. I chose **ribollita**, a hearty Tuscan bread-and-bean stew. It tasted like autumn. Like fireplaces and fallen leaves and the joy of something warm in your chest. The couple beside me were locals celebrating an anniversary. They shared their limoncello with me. We toasted, laughed, swapped stories. I didn't feel like a tourist. I felt like a **guest**.

And then there's **Da Nerbone**, inside Mercato Centrale. More on that later. But let's just say: if you're craving the most comforting roast pork sandwich of your life, **you go there**.

Florence is full of these places—**trattorias and osterias that aren't chasing stars, just tradition.** Where the owner is also the cook. Where the menu

47

hasn't changed in twenty years. Where the food tastes like someone loves you.

A dimly lit trattoria interior—brick walls, mismatched chairs, candles flickering on a checkered tablecloth, with a steaming plate of ribollita in the foreground. A window open to a narrow alley beyond. The vibe is intimate, timeless, local.

In Florence, dining is not just about feeding yourself. It's about **feeling something**. Each bite connects you to centuries of taste, patience, and pride.

Mercato Centrale and Sant'Ambrogio Market Adventures

One of my first mornings in Florence, I found myself at **Mercato Centrale**, drawn by the clatter of crates, the call of vendors, the scent of basil and blood orange. The market is an explosion of color and life—**Florence in full bloom**.

On the ground floor, locals shop for their daily ingredients. Butchers call out daily specials. Cheese sellers offer samples of pecorino wrapped in herbs. The bread stalls are mountains of crusty loaves. I watched a woman pick over fresh artichokes while explaining the best way to cook them to a young American student. He took notes on his phone. She laughed and corrected him.

I bought a small bag of sun-dried tomatoes, two fresh peaches, and a hunk of pecorino. I sat on the steps outside and devoured them in silence.

Upstairs, the market transforms into a **food court like no other**. Artisan stalls serve everything from pizza to pasta to seafood and wine. I ordered a plate of gnocchi al pesto, paired it with a glass of Vermentino, and found a spot overlooking the atrium below. Around me, families feasted, friends clinked glasses, travelers planned their next stops. It was loud, delicious chaos.

A few days later, I discovered **Sant'Ambrogio Market**, tucked away from the tourist track in the eastern part of the city. It felt more *real*. More local. Farmers with dirt on their hands sold heirloom tomatoes the size of apples. The fishmonger wore a blue apron and sang while filleting sea bass. A vendor let me sample her homemade fig jam—and then told me about her childhood in the Tuscan hills.

I bought olives, focaccia, and a slice of pecorino with honey. I sat in the nearby **Piazza Sant'Ambrogio**, watched the world go by, and felt Florence **feed me with more than food**.

A vibrant stall at Sant'Ambrogio Market—colorful vegetables spilling from baskets, hand-labeled jars of honey and jam.

Markets in Florence aren't just for shopping. They're for learning. For connecting. For *tasting the city in its most honest form*.

Florence feeds you with art, with beauty, with history. But also—deeply, richly, joyfully—with **food**. Not the kind you forget once the plate is cleared, but the kind that lingers in your soul. Every meal I had in Florence told me a story. Of a grandmother's kitchen. Of a butcher's morning. Of a vineyard in Chianti. Of a city that believes taste is sacred.

And I believed it too.

Chapter 7
Aperitivo Culture and Cafés of the City

How to Do Aperitivo Like a Local: Times, Places, Etiquette

It took me exactly three days in Florence to fall completely in love with **aperitivo**. I had heard the term before I arrived—maybe in passing, maybe in some glossy article—but I didn't really *know* what it meant until I experienced it on a sun-warmed terrace, with a Campari in one hand and olives in the other, the city glowing gold around me.

Aperitivo is **not just a drink**. It's a ritual. A celebration of doing nothing quickly. A way of winding down and reconnecting, often without a single word. It's the hour when Florence seems to lean back, exhale, and put on her softest light.

Locals don't call it "happy hour." That phrase feels transactional. Aperitivo is more like **the poetry of transition**—from day to evening, from work to leisure, from sunlight to lamplight.

It usually starts around **6:00 p.m.** and stretches lazily into the first notes of night. But it's not just about the time—it's about the **feeling**. You sit. You sip. You talk—

or you don't. You eat something small but delightful. And all the while, you're surrounded by the hum of Florence exhaling its day.

I had my first real aperitivo at **La Ménagère**, a beautifully curated spot near the Duomo where flowers, music, cocktails, and design merge effortlessly. I was seated beneath a canopy of Edison bulbs, a jazz trio playing somewhere in the distance, the scent of lemon and gin swirling in the air. The waiter recommended a **Negroni Sbagliato**—a twist on the Florentine classic with prosecco instead of gin. It arrived with a small wooden board topped with prosciutto, Pecorino Toscano, olives, and crostini with whipped truffle butter. It wasn't a meal. It was a **mood**.

In Florence, aperitivo often comes with **complimentary snacks**, especially in more traditional bars. Some places offer full spreads—little buffets with pasta, salad, mini pizzas, and cured meats. Others keep it simple and elegant: chips, nuts, and good olives. The idea isn't to fill up—it's to slow down. To invite conversation. To make space for reflection.

Some etiquette tips I learned the delicious way:

- **Don't rush.** Aperitivo is not a quick drink before dinner. It *is* the beginning of your evening.

- **Don't order like it's a bar back home.** Ask for recommendations. Say "Vorrei un aperitivo tipico, per favore."
- **Enjoy the pairing.** A spritz without a snack is incomplete. Even the smallest bite enhances the flavor.

Favorite spots for aperitivo? So many. **Ditta Artigianale** in Oltrarno, **Locale Firenze** for something more upscale, **Rasputin** if you want hidden speakeasy vibes. But even the most unassuming bar on a quiet side street can gift you with a magical hour you'll never forget.

Best Cafés for People-Watching and Espresso Moments

There is no better way to understand Florence's rhythm than by sitting at a café and watching the city unfold. It's here, over **a single espresso or a slow cappuccino**, that you begin to feel the heartbeat of the place.

Mornings are sacred. The locals come in waves. No laptops. No to-go cups. Just espresso at the bar, a croissant in hand, and a moment of pause before the world begins. I loved watching it. I'd stand at the marble counter at **Caffè Scudieri** near the Duomo, sip my coffee, and let the aroma wrap around me like silk.

But I'm a writer, a dreamer. So I often lingered longer than any local ever would. That's when I'd find a corner at **Ditta Artigianale**, Florence's answer to the modern café—hip, warm, and filled with everything from freelancers to philosophers. Their flat white is arguably the best in the city, and their banana bread saved me from homesickness more than once.

One afternoon, I took a window seat at **La Cité** in the Oltrarno. I ordered a macchiato and pulled out a book, but found myself watching instead—an older man feeding pigeons near Santo Spirito, a couple arguing in the most theatrical Italian imaginable, a girl sketching the bell tower on a napkin. **Florence is a city of stories**, and cafés are its theaters.

And then, of course, there's the moment when **espresso becomes art**. That happened to me at **Caffè Gilli** in Piazza della Repubblica. One of the oldest cafés in Florence, it still holds the elegance of another time. Waiters in bow ties. Marble counters. Chandeliers. I ordered a caffè corretto—espresso "corrected" with grappa—and watched as a violinist played beneath the carousel outside. I didn't want to leave. I wanted to live in that moment forever.

Here's what I learned: in Florence, **coffee isn't caffeine. It's communion**. With the day. With yourself. With everyone who's sat in that same spot for the past hundred years.

Iconic Bars: Caffè Gilli, Rivoire, Ditta Artigianale
To understand Florence after sunset, you need to spend time in its **iconic bars**—places where time folds in on itself and cocktails become poetry.

Let's start with **Caffè Gilli**, again, because it's not just a café. By evening, it turns into something **shimmering**. The chandeliers cast golden halos on the terrazzo floors, and bartenders stir martinis with old-world flair. I once sat at the bar beside a poet from Naples. We didn't say much, but we toasted quietly with Negronis. That felt enough.

Then there's **Rivoire**, just steps from Palazzo Vecchio. It's always buzzing with life. The terrace gives you a front-row seat to Piazza della Signoria—**David's replica**, street musicians, artists, newlyweds. Their chocolate truffles are legendary. Their cocktails even more so. One rainy night, I ducked inside for a warm drink and found myself at a table with two older Florentines who taught me the phrase *"bere per dimenticare"*—"to drink to forget." We laughed, we drank, and for a moment, I felt like I belonged.

But my personal favorite? **Ditta Artigianale (via dello Sprone)**. A hybrid of old and new. Their bar staff are artists. I had a cocktail there that tasted like summer rain—gin, cucumber, elderflower. Upstairs, a vintage library; downstairs, the hum of music and murmured secrets. I returned three times in one week.

Other spots worth your night:

- **Rasputin**: A speakeasy behind an unmarked wooden door. You knock. You wait. And then you enter velvet-draped mystery and some of the best drinks in Europe.

- **Manifattura**: Where bartenders speak of amari like sommeliers speak of wine.
- **Locale Firenze**: For when you want to dress up and pretend you're in a Renaissance-set James Bond film.

A dimly lit cocktail bar interior—dark wood, flickering candles, a Negroni on a marble counter with condensation glistening

Florentine bars aren't just places to drink. They are **stages of style, emotion, and expression**. Whether you're sipping alone with a journal or clinking glasses in laughter, each one becomes a chapter in your story.

In Florence, **the drink is never just the drink**. The coffee is a pause. The cocktail is a reflection. The aperitivo is a golden hour for the soul. I came here thinking food and wine were accessories to the art and architecture. I was wrong. They *are* the art and architecture—built slowly, tasted deeply, remembered forever.

Aperitivo taught me to slow down. Coffee taught me to look closer. The bars reminded me that even solitude can sparkle if you hold your glass with the right kind of grace.

So sit down. Sip slowly. Watch the light shift. And let Florence rise to meet you—**one small glass at a time**.

Chapter 8
Bars, Clubs, and Florence After Dark

Where to Dance: Otel, Tenax, YAB, and Late-Night Rhythm

Florence may be the cradle of the Renaissance, but come nightfall, it sheds its classical cloak and pulls you into a different kind of art—**the art of the night**. When the museums lock their doors and the sun dips behind the Duomo, a rhythm begins to pulse below the cobblestones. A rhythm that calls to the dancers, the dreamers, the lovers of basslines and neon.

I discovered **Otel** on my first Friday night in the city. Locals spoke about it like a rite of passage. "Go late," they said, "and dress like you mean it." Tucked along the riverbank, just outside the historical core, Otel looked nondescript from the outside—an industrial building tucked among trees and street lamps. But inside? **Velvet, chandeliers, bottle service, and beats that reached into your chest**. The DJ transitioned seamlessly from Italian house to international hits, and the dance floor shimmered with motion. Locals, students, fashion types, and expats mingled as if they'd all grown up on the same street. I stayed until 4 a.m., dancing in a strobe-lit dream, emerging into the cool night air flushed and wide awake.

A few nights later, I craved something rawer—less curated, more electric. I found it at **Tenax**. This isn't a tourist's club. This is **Florence's underground temple of techno**. A warehouse near the airport, dark and loud and beautiful in its intensity. I arrived past midnight and left at sunrise, in between letting the bass swallow me whole. There were no velvet ropes, no VIP lounges— just people moving, eyes closed, bodies honest. It was **Florence unfiltered**, and it felt like freedom.

Then came **YAB**—short for *You Are Beautiful*—a little more central, a little more glam, but with an infectious energy that pulled me in immediately. I went on a Thursday, student night, when the floor was packed with university life from across Europe. Music ranged from reggaeton to Europop to nostalgic 2000s dance. I didn't know anyone when I walked in, but by midnight I was spinning in a circle of strangers-turned-friends, all of us shouting the chorus to a song we hadn't heard in years. That's what Florence does after dark. It

Wine Bars and Speakeasies for Slow Evenings
Not every Florentine night is for dancing. Some are for **savoring**—a slower kind of pleasure, where the night unfolds like a story told glass by glass. Florence knows how to keep it quiet, sensual, and elegant. On those nights, I found myself in **wine bars and hidden**

speakeasies, where conversations run long and music whispers in corners.

The first wine bar I truly fell for was **Le Volpi e L'Uva**, just a few cobblestone steps from Ponte Vecchio. It's small—barely a dozen seats outside—but every bottle behind the bar was selected with love. The staff were more like curators than servers, guiding me through the subtle notes of Tuscan reds and wild Sicilian whites. I sat beneath a soft lantern glow, tasting crostini topped with truffle cream and duck pâté. Strangers spoke in low tones. Laughter punctuated the silence like jazz. It was effortless magic.

Another night led me to **Rasputin**, Florence's most famous speakeasy—though you wouldn't find it unless you knew exactly where to knock. Hidden in Santo Spirito, behind a plain wooden door and a single flickering lantern, Rasputin is candlelit and decadent. The walls are lined in velvet. The bartenders move like stage performers. The drinks? **Alchemy**. I ordered a smoked mezcal cocktail with hints of bergamot and thyme. It tasted like memory—earthy and dark and somehow nostalgic. Around me, couples whispered over crystal glasses, and time slowed like syrup.

Manifattura offered something entirely different— **Florence's love letter to Italian spirits**. Tucked in a quiet street near Piazza di Santa Maria Novella, it served only made-in-Italy liquors. One of the bartenders introduced me to "Vecchio Amaro del Capo," poured over ice with orange peel. "This," he said, "is Italy in winter." And it was. Bittersweet and bold. I stayed past midnight, writing in my notebook and watching the shadows of the bar dance.

Florence's quieter nights are no less rich. They're just **softer, deeper, designed for feeling rather than frenzy**. These are the nights when a glass of wine becomes a bridge—between you and the city, between you and yourself.

LGBTQ+-Friendly Nightlife and Inclusive Spaces
Florence may be steeped in tradition, but it is far from closed. I found **LGBTQ+-friendly nightlife not only present, but thriving—warm, inclusive, and joyful**. In a city of statues and saints, I found glitter and grace.

My first night at **Piccolo Caffè**, near the Duomo, felt like crashing someone's glittering birthday party. The music was campy, loud, and perfect. Madonna, Lady Gaga, ABBA—each song was a celebration. Drag queens danced between tables. The bartender wore a crop top and the biggest smile I'd ever seen. I came alone and left with lipstick on my cheek, three new friends from Milan, and sore legs from dancing. No one cared where you were from or who you loved. You just had to **be open**.

Then came **FLO Lounge**, open in the warmer months in a hilltop garden just above Piazzale Michelangelo. You climb through olive trees to get there, and then suddenly, Florence opens up beneath you—**the city glowing**, the Arno glinting, and house music pulsing under the stars. I went on a themed night—"Queer Garden"—and it was exactly that. Queer. Joyful. Growing. People kissed under trees. Danced in heels on grass. The bartenders wore sequins. The DJ played everything from Donna Summer to Stromae. It was electric and easy and safe.

Inclusivity in Florence isn't confined to queer bars either. One night, I ended up at a poetry reading in a bar in San Frediano. A nonbinary performer read verses about heartbreak and resilience, and the entire crowd—gay, straight, trans, unsure—stood and clapped. The city might be old, but its heart is **expanding**.

Florence gave me something I didn't expect—**a safe space to simply be**. Whether I was dancing in a queer bar, sipping vermouth in a speakeasy, or holding hands on a midnight walk along the Arno, I was met with smiles, nods, and the kind of unspoken acceptance that feels like a deep breath.

Florence after dark is not just one thing. It is many. A mirrored disco ball spinning above a dance floor. A wine-stained napkin scribbled with poetry. A hand reaching across a candlelit table. A drag queen in full sequins quoting Dante between pop songs. A techno beat pounding in a warehouse until sunrise. The glow of lamps in a quiet piazza at 2 a.m. It is all of this and more.

I came for Botticelli. I stayed for the nights when the city shed its skin, lit up from within, and whispered, *You're welcome here. All of you.*

Chapter 9
Shopping and Artisan Streets

Leather Markets, Goldsmiths, and Florentine Craftsmanship

Florence smells like leather. Step off the train at Santa Maria Novella, wander a few blocks into San Lorenzo, and you'll catch it in the air—that rich, buttery scent of tanned hide and beeswax polish, of ancient trades still alive beneath awnings and arches. My first morning wandering the **San Lorenzo leather market**, I felt both dazzled and disoriented. Stalls overflowed with jackets, belts, wallets, and bags in every shade from oxblood to chestnut to ink black. Vendors called out in multiple languages, luring tourists with smiles and soft Italian flattery. It was easy to be swept up in it.

I ran my fingers across buttery-soft bags, watched a woman expertly cut a leather strip, and listened as a merchant explained the difference between cowhide and calfskin. I bought a small hand-stitched journal in burnt sienna—the smell alone was worth the price. It still carries the scent of that day, like Florence itself pressed between its pages.

But the true magic was not in the markets—it was in the **workshops**, tucked behind curtains or down narrow alleys where the real craftspeople worked. In the **Scuola**

del Cuoio (Leather School) inside Santa Croce's monastery, I met a man who had been making bags by hand for over forty years. He showed me his tools: awls, burnishers, bone folders. Every mark he made was with purpose. His hands told the story of a tradition passed down from the Renaissance. "You don't buy a bag," he said. "You inherit it."

Gold, too, is part of Florence's soul. The **goldsmiths of Ponte Vecchio** still shine in their narrow shops, tucked beneath creaking wooden shutters. I stepped into a tiny boutique where the owner's family had been shaping gold for three generations. He showed me a bracelet design inspired by the cornices of Brunelleschi's dome—delicate, architectural, timeless. Every piece of jewelry in Florence seems tied to the land itself. It's not about sparkle. It's about story.

A cobbled alley in San Lorenzo lined with leather stalls—sunlight catching the rich textures of hanging jackets and bags.

Florentine craftsmanship isn't just about aesthetics. It's about honoring time. Every stitch, every curve of gold, every crease in a leather bag carries a piece of the city—**crafted slowly, worn with pride, lasting forever**.

Oltrarno's Artisans: Paper, Perfume, Frames, and Fine Art

Cross the Arno and Florence shifts. The streets grow quieter, the air cooler, and the rhythm of the city slows. **Oltrarno** is where Florence breathes deeply. It's where the tourists thin and the artists linger. My feet led me there instinctively, and I returned again and again—not for monuments, but for makers.

I discovered **paper first**. At Il Papiro on Via dei Bardi, shelves overflowed with marbled journals, hand-printed stationery, wax seals, and pens carved like wands. I watched as a woman swirled dyes through a tray of water, dipped a sheet into the liquid, and lifted it into a riot of emerald and gold. She smiled, noticing my wonder. "No two are the same," she said. "Just like people."

Next came **perfume**—an art form Florence takes seriously. Inside **AquaFlor Firenze**, hidden behind an iron gate near Piazza Santa Croce, I found a vaulted 13th-century chapel-turned-fragrance-lab. The space smelled like dreams—tobacco, iris, leather, fig, rain. A perfumer let me sample a scent she called "Oliveto." One drop on my wrist and I was transported to the Tuscan countryside: olive groves, dusty hills, lavender in the wind. I left with a small bottle that felt like a secret in my pocket. Whenever I wear it, I'm there again.

Art and craft blur constantly in the Oltrarno. I stumbled into **Cornici Galleria L'Ippogrifo**, where a fourth-generation framer shaped wood with monastic focus. Beside him, his daughter gilded a frame using gold leaf so thin it curled in the air like silk. The frame was for a fresco fragment from a nearby chapel—centuries old, now newly honored.

Then came the artists. In **Spazio Nota**, a shared studio and gallery, I met a painter working on miniature landscapes of Florence from memory. "I don't sell views," she said. "I sell feelings." I bought a tiny watercolored square of the Duomo at dusk. It hangs on my wall now, small and brave, like the moment I found it.

The Oltrarno isn't just where things are made. It's where **meaning is shaped**—folded into paper, mixed into scent, gilded into wood, and painted into silence. Florence lives there, not in grand galleries, but in the rhythm of hands and hearts.

Where to Buy Souvenirs with Heart (and How to Avoid Tourist Traps)

Shopping in Florence can be magical—or disappointing—depending on where you look. The city overflows with beauty, but it also **brims with mass-produced souvenirs** designed for hurried travelers. I saw the same Michelangelo magnets, plastic Davids, and imitation leather bags a hundred times. And I almost bought them—until Florence taught me something deeper: *the best souvenir is something that carries someone's time, not just their logo.*

So I made a rule for myself: **If I couldn't speak to the person who made it, I didn't buy it.**

In the historic center, I looked for small storefronts with names on the door. In Oltrarno, I asked locals where they bought gifts. I visited **Bottega Orafa**, a jewelry studio where the goldsmiths were kind enough to explain the technique of *filigrana*. I found **Carta Firenze**, a tiny paper shop near the Duomo, where the owner bound journals with marbled covers and rough-cut pages. And I spent an afternoon in **La Bottega del Chianti**, tasting handmade olive oils and balsamic vinegars from the countryside, choosing bottles not for packaging, but for flavor.

For friends back home, I brought back **pressed flower bookmarks**, linen napkins dyed with saffron, jars of fig jam from Sant'Ambrogio Market, and a tiny hand-carved wooden Pinocchio for my nephew—Florence's most charming puppet.

I avoided the tourist traps by following three simple steps:

- **If it's sold everywhere, it's made nowhere.**
- **If it smells like plastic or looks machine-perfect, it didn't come from Florence.**

- **If the seller tells you a story, listen. If they can't, walk away.**

Souvenirs with heart are the ones that remind you of **a moment, not a shop**. They carry the scent of a workshop, the voice of a maker, the patience of a process. They are the city in your suitcase.

Florence taught me that shopping can be **intimate**, that a scarf or a ring or a bottle of perfume can be more than decoration. It can be a memory made tangible. And when you bring it home, it doesn't just sit on a shelf—it speaks, softly and always, of **a place where things were made with love**.

Chapter 10
Hidden Florence – Secrets and Silence

Quiet Cloisters, Secret Gardens, and Whispering Fountains

Florence has its masterpieces—cathedrals, palaces, piazzas that stun and overwhelm—but some of the most moving encounters I had in the city happened in its **in-between spaces**. The ones you stumble upon accidentally, where silence wraps around you like silk and time feels suspended. My first experience of this quieter Florence was in the cloister of Santa Maria Novella. One moment I was in the bustle of the piazza, and the next I was stepping into a hushed courtyard, the noise falling away like a dropped curtain. The cloister opened before me, all arches and shadows, with pale frescoes on the walls and a patch of garden in the center where a single fountain whispered over stone. I walked slowly, drawn by the rhythm of the water and the flutter of birds in the ivy overhead. The sun filtered in, slanting across the tiled floor in patches. I sat for an hour and didn't speak a word. I didn't need to. The place spoke for itself.

I found more stillness in the **Giardino delle Rose**, tucked just beneath Piazzale Michelangelo. Most tourists stop at the overlook, snap photos of the Duomo, and move on. But if you slip down the steps behind the terrace, you enter a different world—**a terraced rose garden filled with sculpture and silence**. There were lovers curled together on benches, old men reading newspapers in the shade, and a young girl drawing in a sketchbook. I wandered along the gravel paths, past fig trees and stone sculptures by Jean-Michel Folon, and sat by a quiet fountain with a view of the entire city framed in petals and sky. I didn't feel like a visitor anymore. I felt like Florence had taken me in.

Then came the **Bardini Garden**, even more hidden, even more personal. I discovered it by accident while looking for a shortcut to San Niccolò. The entrance was modest, almost secretive, but inside I found terraces climbing gently toward the sky, each turn offering a more breathtaking view than the last. Florence lay below like a living painting, framed by the hush of cypress trees and the sound of bees. At the top, a small stone fountain gurgled into a mossy basin. It was so quiet I could hear my own thoughts taking shape. Bardini wasn't just a garden. It was a retreat, a breath, a long exhale in the middle of history.

Abandoned Towers and Hidden Alleys

Florence is a vertical city—built not just outward, but upward, layer by layer over centuries. Its towers are everywhere if you know where to look, many of them overlooked, **standing like silent witnesses to forgotten feuds and whispered meetings**. One day, I wandered off the Via Calzaiuoli and spotted the **Torre della Castagna**, a tall, narrow stone tower built in the 11th century. Most people passed it by without a glance, but I stopped and imagined what it had seen—medieval battles, cloaked messengers, families watching from the upper windows as fires burned in distant quarters. The city has grown around it, modern shops pressing close, but the tower still stands. Forgotten by many. Remembered by stone.

Even more compelling were the alleys. I became addicted to walking early in the morning, before the crowds emerged, when Florence was still pulling on her cloak. That's when I found her hidden corridors. **Chiasso dei Baroncelli**, near Piazza Signoria, was barely wide enough for a single person. The walls closed in, and yet the light that filtered through made the space glow. I ran my hand along the rough stone and felt Florence's bones.

One of my favorite streets was **Via Toscanella**, tucked in the Oltrarno like a secret. I walked it again and again. A laundry line stretched from window to window. A black cat watched me from a windowsill. The scent of warm bread floated through the air from a tiny bakery at the corner. These alleys weren't tourist routes. They were the city's **veins**, carrying life and memory and moments too small to be listed in any guidebook.

I once wandered into **Via dell'Amorino**, not because I was looking for it, but because I was lost. The name stopped me in my tracks—*Little Love Street*. There was nothing flashy about it. No statue, no plaque. Just stone and shadow and the soft sound of footsteps. But it stayed with me. Because in that moment, I felt Florence lean in and whisper, *This is just for you.*

Convents, Artisan Courtyards, and Places of Stillness

I often found myself slipping into convents—not for religion, but for **peace**. Florence's convents are pockets of silence, where the air feels different and the pace slows to a near stop. I found myself in the **Chiostro dello Scalzo** on a sleepy Tuesday morning. There was no one else there. Just the pale grey frescoes of Andrea del Sarto, painted in soft chiaroscuro, and the sound of my footsteps echoing off stone. It felt like stepping into a dream made entirely of shade and breath. The courtyard was open to the sky, but enclosed in spirit. I stayed for a long time, seated on a stone bench, notebook in hand, not writing—just listening to the quiet.

But the most magical courtyards weren't always attached to churches. They were **artisan courtyards**, hidden behind wooden doors in the Oltrarno. One day, following the faint sound of a hammer tapping metal, I peeked into a courtyard where an old man shaped silver jewelry on a wooden bench beneath a fig tree. Beside him, a young woman stitched leather sandals. They didn't stop to greet me—they just smiled and kept working. I stood in the doorway and watched, aware I was seeing something precious. This wasn't staged. It wasn't curated. It was Florence being Florence—**handmade, slow, deeply human.**

And then, high above the city, I found myself at **San Miniato al Monte** one cool evening. The church is grand, but the space beside it—the cemetery, the monks' garden, the tiny stone cloister—is where the soul of the place lives. I wandered the colonnade as dusk settled, cypress trees swaying gently overhead. A monk passed me without a word, hands folded, gaze lowered. I stood by the wall and looked down at Florence glowing in the twilight. Bells rang below, and I felt something shift. Not awe exactly. **Stillness. Surrender. A kind of sacred quiet.**

Hidden Florence isn't found on maps. It finds you—when you're quiet enough, slow enough, open enough. It's in cloisters where prayers hang in the air, in gardens that bloom behind walls, in alleys that narrow until you forget everything except the present. It's in the slow brush of a leatherworker's hand, the swirl of marbled paper drying in the sun, the hollow hush of a stone stairwell that hasn't echoed with footsteps in centuries. And it's in you, when you let the city move through you—not all at once, but in soft pulses. Florence's greatest treasures don't hang in gilded frames. They wait in silence. In stillness. In the spaces between.

Chapter 11
Romantic Florence for Two

Best Spots for Couples: Gardens, Rooftops, and Strolls

Florence isn't just beautiful—it's **seductive**. The whole city feels like it was designed for lovers. The way the light hits the Arno at sunset. The way the narrow streets bring you physically closer. The way every corner seems to hold a secret just for two. I arrived in Florence alone, but by the second week, I was falling in step with someone who made the city open in a new way. Florence wasn't just a museum anymore. It was **a mood**, soft and slow and deeply romantic.

Our first real moment happened in the **Bardini Garden**, high above the Arno, where wisteria cascades in lavender waves over a pergola path. We walked hand in hand through tunnels of green, stopping now and then to sit on sun-warmed benches, sharing sips of espresso and stories from childhood. Florence lay below like a whispered promise. That view—of the Duomo framed by olive trees and roses—felt like it belonged to us. We didn't speak much. We didn't need to. Sometimes romance isn't in the words—it's in **the hush between them**.

That evening, we found ourselves at **Piazzale Michelangelo**, not for the view (though it was breathtaking), but for the feeling. Street musicians played soft acoustic covers, and people clinked glasses as the sun slid behind the hills. We brought a small bottle of Chianti and a bar of dark chocolate, sat on the stone wall with our legs dangling, and watched as Florence glowed amber and pink beneath the sky. When the last light faded, he looked at me and smiled. "It's like the city's in love with itself," he said. I nodded. "And with us, too."

Later in the week, we made a reservation at a rooftop bar above **Hotel Continentale**, right beside Ponte Vecchio. The terrace was all candlelight and crisp linen, cocktails with citrus peel garnishes and a view of the river threading through the city. The breeze carried the scent of jasmine, and the laughter from tables around us felt like background music to something cinematic. We toasted to nothing in particular. Or maybe to everything.

Florence makes falling in love easy. Not just with someone, but with **the moment you're sharing**. The strolls through dimly lit alleys, the bridges that invite kisses mid-step, the café corners that become sanctuaries. Every detail is a backdrop for intimacy.

Proposal and Honeymoon Inspiration in Historic Settings

If there's a city that feels *made* for declarations of love, it's Florence. There's something about the way history and beauty collide here that makes even the most ordinary moment feel sacred. I met a couple at our guesthouse who had just gotten engaged. "He proposed at sunset in Fiesole," she told me, her voice still dreamy. "The bells rang right after I said yes." I understood completely. Florence wraps moments in meaning.

If I were to propose in Florence, I'd do it on the **steps of San Miniato al Monte**, just as the light breaks over the rooftops. The city is quiet there—no crowds, just the sound of birds and the bells from the valley below. The sun rises behind you and casts golden light on the face of the Duomo. It feels like the world holding its breath.

For honeymoons, Florence offers a thousand ways to say **"we began here."** Mornings spent walking through cloisters hand in hand, afternoons tucked in wine bars or wandering through Boboli's sun-drenched sculptures. Candlelit dinners under 14th-century frescoes. Rooftop jacuzzis in boutique hotels where you can toast the stars with prosecco. I remember standing in the **Rose Garden** again, this time at dusk, watching a newlywed couple take photos among the blooms.

They didn't pose much—they just looked at each other. Florence took care of the rest.

There's even a special kind of intimacy in visiting a place like **Palazzo Vecchio** together—climbing the tower, hearts pounding from exertion and excitement, and reaching the top together to look out at the city, shoulder to shoulder. It's not just romantic. It's **bonding**, layered with symbolism and shared silence.

Florence is a city where time slows, where beauty becomes witness, where love feels carved into every arch and echoed in every footstep. A proposal here isn't just romantic—it becomes a piece of history.

Private Dinners, Art Dates, and Bespoke Couple Activities

The best moments we shared weren't planned. They unfolded slowly, like Florence herself. One afternoon, after hours wandering hand in hand through the Uffizi, we ducked into a tiny trattoria in San Niccolò with only four tables and candlelight flickering against frescoed walls. There was no menu—just the chef listing what was fresh. We had handmade pici with duck ragù and shared a bottle of Brunello. The server brought us limoncello on the house. "You're clearly celebrating something," he said. We were. We didn't say it, but we were.

The city offers endless ways to fall in love through its **art**. We took a painting class together one rainy afternoon in a studio near Santo Spirito. The instructor, an elderly painter named Giovanni, taught us how to grind pigment and stretch canvas. We painted side by side in silence, laughing softly when our attempts at landscape turned abstract. At the end, he took our hands and dipped them in gold paint, leaving two perfect fingerprints on each of our canvases. "Now your work is touched by Florence," he said. It was.

One evening, we booked a **private dinner on a hidden terrace** near Palazzo Pitti. It was part of a pop-up supper club, hosted by a chef and a sommelier who lived in a renovated 15th-century apartment. The view overlooked terracotta rooftops and bell towers. Dinner was five courses of seasonal dishes—zucchini flowers, saffron risotto, bistecca, panna cotta with rosemary syrup—and between courses, they told stories about Florence's culinary secrets. We were with four other couples, but it felt private, tender, timeless.

Later that week, we joined a **nighttime art walk**, led by a local guide who took us through Florence's quiet piazzas, stopping at statues and telling us the romantic myths behind them—Dante and Beatrice, Apollo and Daphne, the Medici loves. We ended by the Arno, candles floating on the river, and the city glowing like a dream. Florence doesn't force love. It **holds it up gently and says, Here. This is yours.**

Florence isn't about grand gestures. It's about the **moments between moments**. The look exchanged in front of a Botticelli. The way your hands brush when reaching for the same peach in the market. The quiet laughter over shared gelato at midnight. Every brick, every streetlamp, every breeze seems to conspire in your favor. And in that space, love isn't a destination. It's a journey—walked slowly, tenderly, step by beautiful step.

Chapter 12
Florence for Families and Kids

Kid-Friendly Museums and Creative Workshops

Florence, with its Renaissance grandeur and deep artistic heritage, may seem like a city for adults at first glance. But the more time I spent walking its cobbled streets with my nieces in tow, the more I discovered its **playful side**, tucked behind frescoed walls and hidden in sunlit courtyards. One of the first places we visited was the **Museo dei Ragazzi**, located in the Palazzo Vecchio itself. The name translates to "Museum for Kids," but it's so much more than that—it's a palace experience through a child's eyes. They don't just tell kids about history—they let them live it. My nieces were outfitted in velvet Renaissance costumes and taken on a theatrical guided tour through the palace's chambers. Watching them chase the "Duke" through the grand halls, giggling and asking questions about armor and royal feasts, I felt the dusty past become vivid and new. It wasn't a lecture—it was an adventure. And that, I realized, is how you teach children in Florence.

From there, we moved to the **Leonardo da Vinci Museum**, a place that still stands out vividly in our memories. This museum isn't about paintings—it's about **invention**. Full of interactive wooden models of Leonardo's designs, it lets children (and curious adults) turn cranks, pull levers, and lift weights just as the Renaissance genius intended. My nephew spent a solid 30 minutes working the tank replica, while I tried my hand at a flying machine that looked part bird, part dream. There was no shushing, no tiptoeing—just pure, hands-on learning. I watched as children built bridges without nails, spun gears, and saw engineering as magic. Florence wasn't just educating them—it was **igniting their curiosity**.

We also found joy in smaller, lesser-known places, like **La Specola**, the Museum of Natural History, which might not be on every tourist list but should be if you have kids. This place is a labyrinth of animal models and anatomical wax figures—fascinating, a little eerie, and totally unforgettable. The taxidermy rooms, full of lions, birds, and jungle creatures, were like stepping into a time capsule of exploration. My oldest niece, who dreams of being a vet, was mesmerized by the ancient display cases, pointing at each animal and reading the labels out loud.

But perhaps the most delightful surprise came during an afternoon we spent in a workshop near Santo Spirito. We had signed up for a **paper marbling class**, not knowing what to expect. It turned out to be one of the most beautiful family experiences I've ever had. The studio was filled with vats of colored pigments, trays of swirling patterns, and sheets of handmade paper hanging to dry. Our instructor, a soft-spoken artisan with ink-stained hands, showed us how to sprinkle paint on water and shape it with combs and breath. My youngest niece was nervous at first, afraid she'd mess it up. But by the end, she had created three stunning sheets and was asking if she could stay and apprentice. Florence hadn't just entertained her—it had **empowered** her.

Parks, Puppet Shows, and Space to Roam

While museums fed their minds, the kids also needed to stretch, laugh, run, and breathe. Luckily, Florence has green spaces tucked in and around its historic core that feel like small sanctuaries. Our favorite by far was the **Boboli Gardens**, which offers wide open spaces for running and exploration beneath statues and fountains. We brought a picnic—fresh schiacciata bread, olives, strawberries—and found a shaded spot near the Neptune Fountain. As I lay on the grass, watching the kids chase each other through the hedge mazes and climb the gentle slopes, I realized that Florence doesn't need a playground to be fun. The garden itself is a playground—if you know how to see it that way.

Another favorite was the **Cascine Park**, Florence's largest public park and a true breath of fresh air. Here, away from the Renaissance crush, the kids rented bikes and zoomed down wide paved paths while we followed on foot. There were food trucks selling gelato and crepes, and a carousel that made my younger niece scream with joy. On Tuesday mornings, the park hosts a local market where we picked up fresh strawberries, postcards, and even a hand-painted kite. That afternoon we flew it by the riverbank, laughter rising with each gust of wind. It felt like **pure freedom**.

We stumbled upon a **puppet show** in Piazza della Repubblica quite by accident one evening. A small stage had been set up, and children gathered on the stone steps, eyes wide. The puppeteer was animated and full of character voices, speaking in both Italian and English. The story was about Pinocchio—a perfect choice in the land of Collodi. My nephew, who rarely sits still for anything, sat entranced, mouthing the lines and cheering when Pinocchio outwitted the fox. It was spontaneous, old-fashioned fun, the kind that doesn't need technology—just imagination and heart.

On another day, we visited the **Stibbert Park**, a place off the usual tourist path. It surrounds a quirky museum filled with suits of armor, but outside it's all winding trails, forested corners, and gentle hills. The kids turned it into an enchanted forest, inventing stories about knights and dragons as they played among the trees.

There were no signs, no crowds, just nature doing what it does best—inviting us to **imagine**.

Family Restaurants and Gelato Stops Children Will Love

Feeding children in a foreign city can be tricky, but in Florence, it's delightfully simple. Every trattoria and osteria we visited welcomed children like honored guests. There were crayons on the table, half-sized portions without even asking, and servers who crouched down to eye level to take their order. One of our go-to spots was **Trattoria ZaZa**, near the Mercato Centrale. They served steaming plates of gnocchi, pizzas big enough for two, and the most tender chicken Milanese I've ever had. The kids loved the fried zucchini flowers—light, crispy, and surprisingly fun to dip.

Another gem was **La Ménagère**, a dreamy space that combines café, florist, and restaurant all in one. At first, I thought it might be too elegant for kids, but they adored it. They watched the flower arrangements being made, marveled at the pink ceiling, and devoured their mini pancakes and berry juice. For me, it was a rare moment of aesthetic beauty and calm, shared with my family over breakfast pastries and cappuccinos.

And then, of course, there was the **gelato**. Florence doesn't do ice cream. Florence does *art in a cone*. Every evening became a mini-adventure—**which gelateria tonight?** We sampled at least a dozen over our stay, but favorites included **Gelateria dei Neri** (for pistachio and stracciatella), **La Carraia** (perfectly creamy mango), and **Vivoli**, one of the oldest in the city. Watching the kids choose their flavors—usually at least two each—became a highlight of every day. Sometimes we'd sit on a bench in Piazza Santa Croce, sticky fingers and chocolate smiles, watching the sun set. Other times we'd stroll along the Arno, cones in hand, sharing bites and swapping spoons. It wasn't just dessert—it was ritual.

We also found that Florence offers **cooking classes for families**, where kids get to knead pasta dough, roll out tagliatelle, and decorate their own pizzas. In one kitchen near Piazza della Signoria, the chef had the children don aprons and chef hats, and the joy on their faces as they pulled bubbling pizzas from the oven was unforgettable. My nephew made a Margherita that he proudly called "the best in Italy." I couldn't disagree.

Florence for families isn't just about keeping kids entertained. It's about seeing the city **through their eyes**. In the laughter that echoed through museums, in the stories they made up while exploring gardens, in the joy of finding the perfect scoop of gelato, Florence became more than a destination. It became a **memory**

palace, layered with laughter, curiosity, flavor, and love. For a parent, an aunt, a grandparent, or a guardian, Florence offers something precious—**not just time spent together, but time deeply shared**. And that, in the end, is the greatest journey of all.

Chapter 13
Faith, Religion, and Cultural Rituals

The Catholic Heartbeat: Daily Rituals, Bells, and Mass

Florence breathes with a rhythm you can't always see, but you can hear it—**in the ringing of bells**, in the low murmur of prayers echoing through stone churches, in the way people pause instinctively when a priest passes in the street. Even if you're not religious, it's impossible to spend time in this city and not feel its **spiritual heartbeat** pulsing beneath your feet.

My first morning in Florence, I was jolted awake by a bell—clear, resonant, ancient. It wasn't the kind of alarm that fades into the background. It felt like a call. I leaned out the window of my pensione near Santa Croce and listened. One chime, then another, then dozens overlapping in waves. The sound rolled across the terracotta rooftops like incense. I would come to learn these bells—**from the Giotto campanile, from San Lorenzo, from San Miniato al Monte**—and the way they stitched the day together like a liturgical thread.

On Sunday, I wandered into **Santa Maria Novella** just as Mass was beginning. I hadn't planned it, but Florence has a way of drawing you inward when you least expect it. I took a seat near the back, beneath a frescoed ceiling that seemed to hum with centuries of devotion. Latin rose into the air. Candles flickered. A woman beside me made the sign of the cross with a grace that seemed choreographed. I didn't understand every word, but I understood the silence between them. It was peace. It was ritual. It was the city **remembering who she is**.

Even outside the churches, the presence of faith is constant. I saw shopkeepers pause at noon to step outside and bow their heads as bells rang the Angelus. I passed elderly women in black, lighting candles at shrines built into street corners—small alcoves holding painted Madonnas, usually framed in flowers, always glowing softly. It wasn't performative. It was personal. Quiet. Woven into the rhythm of life.

A soft-lit interior of Santa Maria Novella during morning Mass—sunlight streaming through stained glass

Florence's Catholicism isn't just historical—it's **alive**, in the footsteps of pilgrims, the scent of wax and stone, and the ancient bells that remind the city, hour by hour, to pause and look up.

Patron Saint Festivals and Religious Processions
I didn't fully grasp how **deeply Florence celebrates its faith** until I witnessed the festival of **San Giovanni Battista**, the city's patron saint. June 24th started like any other summer day—hot, bright, full of tourists. But by late morning, the air had changed. Piazza del Duomo filled with people dressed in Renaissance garb—drummers, flag bearers, priests in golden vestments.

They gathered in solemn formation and began to move through the streets, flanked by crowds holding olive branches and cell phones in equal measure. The city wasn't performing. The city was **participating**, as it has for centuries.

The procession passed beneath my balcony. I watched in silence as the relics of San Giovanni were carried through the city by white-gloved hands. The sound of drums and incense filled the air. Along the streets, shopkeepers closed their doors and stood quietly as the procession moved by. It wasn't a show. It was **respect**. History and belief folded into a single moment. Later that evening, the city celebrated with fireworks over the Arno—explosions of color mirrored in the river, and the bells of every church ringing out in joy.

Smaller festivals carried the same weight. I stumbled upon a **Corpus Domini procession** near Santo Spirito, unannounced and entirely local. A group of children in white robes scattered flower petals ahead of a priest carrying the Eucharist under a canopy of gold. People knelt on the sidewalk. Others watched from windows above. The silence was deeper than any cathedral. I found myself holding my breath. It wasn't about doctrine—it was about **devotion**. The kind that lives in the body and soul, passed down like a lullaby.

During Easter, the city's most famous ritual takes place: the **Scoppio del Carro**—the Explosion of the Cart. On Easter Sunday morning, a cart filled with fireworks is pulled through the city by oxen, accompanied by musicians, clergy, and costumed guards. It's parked in front of the Duomo, and during Mass, a mechanical dove—called the *colombina*—flies down a wire and ignites the cart. The explosion is meant to ensure a good harvest and divine favor for the city. The crowd erupts in cheers. The tradition is over 350 years old, and it still brings tears to people's eyes. Watching it, I felt like I was standing not in a city, but in a **living tapestry**.

A San Giovanni procession in full color—drummers and flag bearers in medieval garb marching past the Duomo. In Florence, faith doesn't stay inside churches. It **moves**, in the streets, in the festivals, in the hearts of people who still believe that tradition isn't old—it's eternal.

Religion in Everyday Life: Icons, Gestures, and Respect

What surprised me most in Florence wasn't the grandeur of its cathedrals, but the **everyday holiness** woven into its smallest details. The sacred lives here not in grand declarations, but in gestures so quiet you might miss them if you weren't paying attention. Like the flicker of a hand making the sign of the cross when a bell rings. Or the way a mother teaches her child to genuflect before sitting in the pew. These aren't acts of obligation. They're acts of **intimacy**.

Walking through the city, I began to notice the **street shrines**—small altars built into the walls, usually near intersections or above doorways. Some are ornate, with painted saints and glass lanterns. Others are so simple—a faded print of the Virgin Mary, a flower pot, a flickering candle. Locals pass them without fanfare, but I often saw them glance up, nod slightly, or whisper something as they walked by. A private moment of connection. A reminder of something larger than the day.

Even the language reflects this quiet reverence. *Dio mio, Madonna santa, Per l'amor di Dio*—phrases of frustration and wonder that root emotion in the divine. It's not blasphemy. It's **recognition**—that joy and sorrow, like prayer, are part of daily life. I watched shopkeepers touch their lips and press their fingers to icons near their cash registers. I saw taxi drivers trace a cross on their steering wheels before turning the key. Faith wasn't reserved for Sunday. It was lived—softly, steadily, lovingly.

Florence also taught me how to **enter a sacred space**. Not just physically, but emotionally. You don't talk on the phone in a chapel. You lower your voice when bells ring. You don't take selfies at the altar. You step lightly on marble worn by devotion. Even if you don't believe, you **respect**. That's the unwritten contract here.

One afternoon, I sat in the side chapel of Santa Croce. A woman came in, knelt, and began to cry. No one stared. No one interrupted. The silence made space for her. That's what Florence does. It **honors the private within the public**, gives you room to feel whatever you need to feel, in the presence of something sacred.

Florence taught me that religion isn't just something you practice. It's something you **carry**—in your gestures, in your language, in the way you move through the world. Faith isn't loud here. It doesn't shout. It hums, like a memory half-remembered, like the scent of incense on an old robe, like the sound of bells calling you home.

Chapter 14
Festivals, Holidays, and Local Celebrations

Scoppio del Carro (Explosion of the Cart) and Easter Traditions

Florence is a city of ritual. It doesn't just observe traditions—it lives inside them. And nowhere is this more vivid, more alive, than in its celebration of **Easter morning**, when the centuries-old ritual of the **Scoppio del Carro**, or "Explosion of the Cart," transforms Piazza del Duomo into something otherworldly. I had read about it before arriving, but nothing could prepare me for what it felt like to stand in that square, surrounded by bells, incense, and the crackling anticipation of a city waiting for something both ancient and electric. I arrived early—just after sunrise—joining the crowd as it gathered along the cathedral steps. There was a murmur in the air, the kind of hush that only comes when people are sharing in something sacred. The **cart itself** stood tall and proud in the piazza—a towering, flower-draped structure pulled by two majestic white oxen, their horns wreathed in spring blossoms. A procession of officials in Renaissance costume passed through the crowd, bearing banners and torches, their faces solemn, their movements rehearsed and reverent. At the height of the Easter Mass, as the Archbishop raised the host, the mechanical dove—the *colombina*—was ignited at the altar and flew along a wire from the Duomo to the cart outside. The crowd held its breath. And then—**boom.** Fireworks exploded in a dazzling spectacle of light, smoke, and color, sending pigeons into the sky and joy cascading through the piazza. The bells of Giotto's campanile rang out in a chaotic chorus, and people cheered, laughed, cried. It wasn't just a display. It was a **blessing**, believed to ensure a good harvest and spiritual prosperity for Florence in the year ahead. In that moment, history wasn't something behind glass—it was flying through the air above our heads, blazing across the Tuscan sky.

The entire Easter season in Florence is marked by this blend of spectacle and intimacy. On Holy Thursday, I visited the **Duomo for the washing of the feet**—a quiet, candlelit service where the archbishop reenacts Christ's gesture of humility. On Good Friday, the streets grew somber. Shops dimmed their lights. And then came Sunday, bursting with resurrection energy, Florence at its most luminous. What touched me most was how this wasn't just for tourists. It was for **the people of Florence**, who bring their children, who stand in the rain if necessary, who take the tradition personally. It reminded me that celebration isn't always about noise. Sometimes it's about **continuity**, the sacred thread that ties past to present with the strength of collective memory.

A wide shot of Piazza del Duomo during the Scoppio del Carro, the cart mid-explosion in golden daylight, with crowds cheering, confetti in the air, and the Duomo's marble façade glowing behind it. The image should feel historic, joyful, and kinetic.

Calcio Storico: Florence's Historical Sport with Passion

When I first heard about **Calcio Storico**, I thought it was a joke. "It's like football," someone told me, "but with medieval costumes and punching." I laughed—until I saw it for myself. Held every June in Piazza Santa Croce, Calcio Storico is not just a sporting event. It's **a battle, a tradition, a public ritual of identity**. I showed up hours before kickoff, and the piazza was already buzzing. Sand had been poured over the cobblestones. The stands were packed with locals dressed in neighborhood colors—red for Santa Maria Novella, blue for Santa Croce, green for San Giovanni, and white for Santo Spirito. It wasn't touristy. It was tribal. I could feel the tension in the air—**this was not just a game**.

The procession began with trumpets and flag-throwers, drummers in velvet tunics, and men bearing spears and banners. The players entered like warriors, bare-chested and tattooed, some already bleeding from warm-up skirmishes. When the whistle blew, chaos erupted. Thirty minutes of punching, grappling, sprinting, tackling, and scoring—**a cross between rugby, wrestling, and ancient warfare**. The crowd roared with every move. I saw mothers scream support, old men weep when a goal was scored, teenagers chanting their neighborhood names like battle cries.

But within the chaos, there was also **discipline**. The players weren't just brawling—they were honoring centuries of Florentine identity. This tradition dates back to the 16th century, when noblemen played to prove their strength. Today, it's a way for the city's *rioni*—its historic districts—to assert pride and passion. After the match, I followed a parade back into the narrow streets, where drums continued to beat and players, limping and grinning, were hailed like gladiators. It was violent, yes—but it was also poetic in its intensity, a kind of **visceral history you could feel in your bones**.

Pitti Uomo, Christmas Lights, and Summertime Street Festivals

Not all of Florence's celebrations are centuries old. Some are thoroughly modern, yet rooted in the same spirit of **elegance, drama, and flair**. In January and again in June, Florence transforms into a fashion epicenter for **Pitti Uomo**, one of the world's most prestigious menswear events. I happened to be there during the summer edition. I was walking through Piazza Ognissanti when I saw them—**men in perfectly tailored suits**, linen and silk fluttering in the breeze, pocket squares folded like origami. The whole city became a runway. Cafés overflowed with designers, editors, models, and photographers. Even the locals dressed sharper. There were runway shows in Renaissance palaces, parties in hidden gardens, art exhibitions tied to fabric and form. What struck me was how Florence took it in stride. This wasn't a city trying to be cool. It **already was**—in its bones. I visited the Museo Ferragamo and saw how deeply fashion and Florence were linked—how design here isn't a trend, but a philosophy. Watching the Pitti crowd strut beneath frescoed ceilings, I realized: **Florence doesn't follow fashion. It shapes it.**

When winter comes, the city **glows**. From early December, lights bloom across Via Tornabuoni and the Duomo is lit like a jewel. I spent a December evening wandering through the **Weihnachtsmarkt**, the German-style Christmas market in Piazza Santa Croce. Wooden stalls sold mulled wine, ornaments, candles, and bratwurst. A carousel spun in the background, and somewhere nearby, a choir sang carols in Italian. The scent of cinnamon and roasted chestnuts followed me like perfume. I bought handmade toys and a wool scarf, watched couples kiss beneath garlands, and felt that old holiday magic I thought I'd outgrown. Florence gave it back to me.

And then there are the **summer nights**, when the city becomes one long street festival. From **Festa di San Lorenzo** in August, with its free pasta dinners and all-night concerts in the piazza, to smaller *sagre* in neighborhoods like San Frediano, where I once danced to live jazz beneath string lights and drank wine with people I'd only just met. The streets fill with laughter and clinking glasses. Projection art lights up the Ponte Vecchio. There are film screenings in cloisters, pop-up dinners in courtyards, open-air operas at night. You don't need tickets—you just need to **wander and follow the sound of joy**.

Florence doesn't celebrate like other cities. It **weaves its identity into celebration**, so that every festival—whether sacred, savage, stylish, or sweet—feels like a piece of its soul shared openly with the world. From the firework-streaked skies of Easter to the pounding drumbeat of Calcio Storico, from the elegance of silk lapels to the warmth of holiday lights, Florence doesn't just mark time—it **inhabits it fully**, gloriously, unapologetically. Being part of its celebrations means becoming part of its history. And there's no greater invitation than that.

Chapter 15
Florence by Season

Spring: Wisteria Blooms, Garden Walks, and Easter Magic

Florence in spring is a city waking up gently, stretching its limbs beneath clear blue skies, and dressing itself in soft colors and floral perfume. I arrived one April afternoon when the air was warm enough to shed a coat but still carried the coolness of winter in the shadows. The streets were brighter, the cafes fuller, and the sky over the Arno shimmered like a freshly cleaned canvas. The first thing I noticed was the **wisteria**. It spilled over garden walls and iron gates, twisting in lavender clouds along the pergolas of Bardini Garden. I walked beneath those vines, each bloom brushing my shoulder like a whisper. The garden was alive—bees drifting between tulips and camellias, birdsong tumbling from trees. And below, Florence stretched out in sunlight, the Duomo glowing white against a soft blue sky. Everything smelled new, hopeful, reborn.

Spring is when Florence's gardens become sanctuaries. I returned often to **Giardino delle Rose**, where roses in every shade lit up the terraced hillside. There was a couple painting quietly beneath an olive tree, and an old woman feeding birds from a brown paper bag. On Easter morning, I joined locals in Piazza del Duomo for

Scoppio del Carro, Florence's explosive blessing of spring. The crowd was electric. People filled balconies, children waved flags, and the air smelled of incense and fire. When the dove flew and the cart erupted into fireworks, it felt like the city itself was rejoicing in the return of light. Later, I sat at a café on Via dei Servi, watching families stroll in their Sunday best, and thought: spring in Florence isn't just a season—it's **a soft crescendo**, where everything begins again.

A wisteria-draped pergola path in Bardini Garden during full bloom.

Summer: Sun-Soaked Piazzas, Longer Days, and Evening Life

By June, the city changes. The sun climbs higher, the streets buzz longer, and Florence radiates with **heat and life**. I arrived for the summer solstice one year, and within minutes I was blinking in the brightness, my sandals clicking on cobblestones warmed like bricks from an oven. Mornings started early, with espresso standing at the bar before the sun became too bold. The city was already moving—markets spilling into streets, children chasing pigeons in Piazza della Repubblica, artists setting up easels along the Arno.

Afternoons in summer were slow, heavy with sun and scent. I'd escape into the cool shadows of **Santa Maria Novella** or sip lemon granita beneath a café awning in Oltrarno. The best hours, though, came in the evening. As the light softened and shadows grew long, Florence transformed into a **theatre of golden glow**. Locals strolled the **Lungarno**, hand in hand, as buskers played soft jazz and the river glimmered like melted bronze. I once watched a wedding couple kiss beneath the lanterns of Ponte Santa Trinita as the city around them exhaled.

Summer also means celebration. I attended **Calcio Storico** in Piazza Santa Croce—a blur of color, sand, shouting, and pride. Then came **Festa di San Giovanni**, Florence's patron saint's day, with medieval processions by day and **fireworks over the Arno** by night. That night, I lay on my back in Piazzale Michelangelo with strangers who felt like friends, the city lit beneath us and sparks cascading above. The air smelled of jasmine and sweat, wine and fireworks. Florence in summer is intense, theatrical, unabashed. She demands your full attention. And you give it willingly.

Autumn and Winter: Truffle Season, Holiday Markets, and Quiet Beauty

When the first cool winds sweep through Florence in October, the city shifts again. The crowds thin, the light softens, and Florence becomes **introspective**. I remember the first time I felt that seasonal hush—I was walking down Via dei Neri and noticed how the leaves from the plane trees had turned gold and were drifting into the Arno. The city smelled different—**earthy, woody, laced with roasted chestnuts**. Autumn here isn't loud. It's **luminous**.

October brought **truffle season**, and every trattoria I entered seemed to echo with the scent of white truffle shaving over handmade pasta. I joined a small group for a truffle-hunting tour just outside the city, walking through damp woods with a trained dog named Luna. When she found one, the guide held it like a sacred object—mud-caked, fragrant, priceless. That night, we feasted on truffle tagliatelle and Chianti, the candlelight catching the steam rising from our bowls like incense.

As the days shortened, the city wrapped itself in warmth. By late November, Florence began to **sparkle**. Strings of lights bloomed across Via Tornabuoni, and shop windows filled with nativity scenes, golden stars, and red velvet. The German-style **Weihnachtsmarkt** in Piazza Santa Croce opened with stalls selling mulled wine, handmade ornaments, toys, and gingerbread. One evening, I watched a child press his nose to a glass jar of sugared almonds while his grandmother sipped hot cider beside him. There were carolers beneath the statue of Dante. The sky was cold and silver. I'd never seen a city look so much like a snow globe.

Then came December, and Florence became **quiet, sacred, and beautiful in its stillness**. I slipped into churches warmed by candlelight, where choirs rehearsed carols in Latin and Italian. On Christmas Eve, I sat in the back of the Duomo for midnight Mass, surrounded by families, flickering votives, and the scent of pine. As the choir sang *Adeste Fideles*, I looked up at the Brunelleschi dome and felt, once again, that in Florence, time folds in on itself—old and new held in the same breath.

Florence by season isn't just about weather—it's about **mood, movement, and memory**. Spring breathes in hope. Summer dances in light. Autumn whispers in gold. Winter folds you into candlelit silence. No matter when you come, Florence meets you exactly as you are—and gives you exactly what you didn't know you needed.

Chapter 16
Day Trips and Tuscan Escapes

Siena, Pisa, and the Chianti Wine Region

Florence, for all her beauty, is only one jewel in the vast crown of Tuscany. From her historic heart, **other worlds unfold** just beyond the city's reach—rolling vineyards, medieval hill towns, cities that glow with the same golden light but hum with different rhythms. I remember waking early one morning with a train ticket in my hand and Siena on my mind. The ride was quiet, misty fields drifting past the window, and then suddenly—**a city of stone and silence**, perched like a crown atop its hill.

Siena felt ancient in a different way from Florence. It breathed slower. The streets curled and narrowed, drawing me toward the shell-shaped **Piazza del Campo**, which opened like a secret. I stood there as the morning bells rang from **Torre del Mangia**, casting long shadows over ochre walls. I wandered into the **Duomo of Siena**, and gasped at the striped marble, the deep greens and blacks, the floor inlaid with sacred stories and pagan symbols. There was less grandeur than Florence, maybe—but more intimacy. More hush. I sat on the steps with a slice of ricciarelli almond pastry and thought, *Florence teaches you art; Siena teaches you reverence.*

Later in the week, I made my pilgrimage to **Pisa**. Yes, the tower leans. But the real miracle is how the entire **Piazza dei Miracoli** feels like it belongs to another realm. The white marble glowed against a sky so blue it looked painted. Tourists posed at every angle, arms outstretched, but I wandered behind the Baptistery, where few people go, and sat in the quiet grass. Inside the cathedral, I lit a candle. I touched the ancient stone and felt its coolness in my palm. Pisa, for all its fame, still had pockets of stillness.

But the most unforgettable escape came in the form of **Chianti**. One sunny Wednesday, I rented a Vespa with a friend and we rode south through winding roads that carved through the hills like ribbon. Vineyards stretched to the horizon, olive groves silver-green and rustling in the breeze. We stopped in **Greve in Chianti**, where the piazza smelled of pecorino and wild herbs. At a nearby winery, we were welcomed by an old man with a sun-leathered face and a heart full of hospitality. He poured us wine the color of garnets and told us stories of his grandfather's vines. The air was thick with lavender. The hills glowed. That day, Tuscany felt like a memory I hadn't lived yet—but somehow already missed.

A sun-drenched vineyard in Chianti at golden hour, with rows of vines disappearing into the hills, a rustic stone farmhouse in the background.

Chianti, Siena, and Pisa offer more than just sights—they offer **textures**, flavors, silences, and stories. They remind you that Tuscany is not a place you visit. It's a place you **feel your way through**.

Lucca and Fiesole: Hilltowns with Heart
Florence sits in the cradle of hills, and in those hills lie towns that feel like echoes—smaller, quieter, more personal, yet just as filled with poetry. I discovered **Lucca** on a gray morning in October, stepping off the train and walking beneath stone gates into a city wrapped in Renaissance walls. Unlike other towns,

Lucca didn't push her beauty on you. She let you find it, slowly. I rented a bicycle and rode the **tree-lined ramparts**, circling the entire city from above, looking down at red-tiled roofs, secret gardens, and chiming towers. Couples strolled hand-in-hand. Children played. Every turn brought a new corner of calm.

Within the walls, I found quiet churches, antique bookshops, and the birthplace of Puccini. I wandered into a music rehearsal in the **Church of San Giovanni**—a soprano practicing "O mio babbino caro"—and my breath caught in my chest. I sat in the pews and wept a little, not from sadness but from the kind of beauty that sneaks up on you and **undoes something inside**. In the afternoon, I sipped hot chocolate on **Piazza dell'Anfiteatro**, watching the elliptical square come alive with soft chatter, laundry hanging, café laughter. Lucca didn't try to impress me. She just **welcomed me quietly**. And that was enough.

Closer to Florence, perched just above her rooftops, is the hillside town of **Fiesole**. I walked there once, in the early morning, climbing past olive groves and villas until Florence fell away behind me like a dream. Fiesole is smaller than you think, but it carries the air of ancient wisdom. I visited the **Roman amphitheater**, silent and moss-covered, and imagined the lives played out there.

I wandered the Etruscan ruins, sat beneath a cypress, and watched fog lift over the valley like a curtain rising.

From the **Monastery of San Francesco**, I looked down at Florence—her dome catching sunlight, her river winding like silk. A nun passed me and smiled. I whispered thanks, though I wasn't sure to whom. Fiesole reminded me that sometimes the best view of something is from **just a little distance**.

Lucca and Fiesole don't dazzle. They **enfold** you, gently. They ask for no more than your quiet attention—and in return, they offer clarity, quiet, and a kind of gentle joy that lingers long after you leave.

Tips for Taking Trains, Buses, or Car Rentals from Florence

Exploring Tuscany from Florence is both simple and soul-enriching—**if you know how to do it right**. I learned early that trains were my best friend. **Santa Maria Novella station**, Florence's main rail hub, is clean, efficient, and incredibly well-connected. For Siena, Pisa, and Lucca, I booked my tickets either online via Trenitalia or directly at the station. It's always best to validate regional tickets at the green machines before boarding—skip that, and you risk a fine, no matter how innocent the mistake. The trains themselves were comfortable, scenic, and on time more often than not. I loved sitting by the window, watching vineyards and cypress trees slide by like paintings come to life.

For towns like Greve in Chianti or smaller wine villages, buses run regularly but often require a bit more planning. I used the **BusItalia service** and picked up timetables from the info booth at the station. Buses are slower, but they take you through tiny hamlets you'd never see otherwise—stone walls covered in ivy, hilltop chapels, roadside fruit stands that look like still lifes. I once struck up a conversation with an elderly woman who told me, "You only find real Tuscany when you're not in a hurry." She was right.

Renting a car offered the most freedom—and some of the most exhilarating drives of my life. The roads between Florence and Chianti felt made for movies, all curves and hills and heart-fluttering vistas. I rented a tiny Fiat 500 for two days and mapped my route through Castellina, Radda, and Volpaia. Parking was often tight in the villages, and gas stations could be few and far between, so I kept a printed map on hand just in case GPS failed. It was worth it for the flexibility—to pull over when the light hit the vines just right, or when a roadside trattoria called my name. Driving through Tuscany gave me something the trains couldn't: **freedom to follow whim and wonder.**

For Fiesole, the simplest escape of all, I often took the #7 **bus** from Piazza San Marco. It winds up the hill and deposits you in another world in just 20 minutes. From there, the best thing to do is walk—slowly, without agenda.

Whether by train, bus, or car, the key to Tuscan travel is this: **don't rush**. Tuscany doesn't like to be hurried. It reveals itself best when you go slowly—when you take the long way, stop for a slice of pecorino, talk to the stranger on the next bench. Florence is a gem, but the land around her is a tapestry. And day by day, road by road, you learn to read it—not with your eyes, but with your soul.

Chapter 17
Practical Travel Tips and Street Smarts

How to Navigate Florence: Walking, Taxis, Scooters, Buses

The best way to understand Florence is on foot. There's no getting around it—**Florence is a walking city**, and her treasures are best discovered at the pace of your own footsteps. My days there always began the same way: espresso in a tiny café, map folded in my bag, and comfortable shoes on my feet. From the Duomo to Santa Croce, from San Lorenzo to Santo Spirito, no place is more than a thirty-minute stroll. And every route brings unexpected joy—a painted doorway, a florist spilling roses onto the street, the smell of fresh schiacciata baking behind an open window.

Florence's medieval layout means that the streets don't always make sense, and you'll get lost at least once. But I promise, that's part of the charm. I got turned around in Oltrarno trying to find a leather workshop, only to stumble upon a cloister I hadn't meant to see. That detour became the best part of my day. Trust your instincts. Let the bells be your compass. And don't be afraid to look up—**signs in Florence live on the walls above you**, not always at eye level.

Taxis are useful but not always obvious. You can't hail one in the street like in New York. Instead, go to designated taxi stands—outside train stations, major piazzas, or call ahead using a local taxi app like It Taxi or Taxi4242. The drivers are generally courteous, though they may not speak much English. Just show your address clearly or have it saved in your phone. They don't expect tips, but rounding up is appreciated.

If you're feeling brave, try a **Vespa or scooter rental**. I rented one for a day to explore beyond the city, and while the initial acceleration made my heart pound, I quickly fell in love with the freedom. Florence's historic center isn't ideal for scooters due to limited ZTL (Zona a Traffico Limitato) areas, but once you're outside the core, the roads open up. A ride through the Tuscan hills in the golden hour—wind in your hair, vineyards passing in a blur—feels like a scene from a Fellini film.

For those wanting an affordable and local alternative, **Florence's buses** run regularly and efficiently. The ATAF bus system connects all major neighborhoods, and tickets can be bought at tabacchi shops (look for the "T" sign), newsstands, or vending machines. Validate your ticket when you board. I used the #7 bus often to reach Fiesole and enjoyed the view as the city fell away behind me.

A winding Florentine street at sunrise—narrow cobblestones leading toward the Duomo, a lone walker with a bag slung over one shoulder.

Florence rewards the traveler who walks slowly, who knows when to hop a bus, and who dares to take the long way home. Getting around isn't just about directions—it's about **letting the city lead you**.

Common Tourist Mistakes and How to Avoid Them
I've made every mistake in Florence. I've shown up at a trattoria without a reservation. I've ordered a cappuccino after lunch. I've stood in line for tickets I should've booked online. The beauty of these mistakes is that they taught me how to travel **better, slower, smarter**—and how to let the city unfold on its own terms.

The most common misstep? **Rushing.** Florence isn't meant to be crammed into 48 hours. You'll miss the rhythm, the in-between moments, the unexpected side streets where the real magic lives. I once watched a group of tourists race past the Duomo on their way to a tour, missing the golden light that hit the dome just as bells began to ring. Slow down. Let yourself be still. One good hour in a piazza is worth more than five frantic check-ins on a bucket list.

Another big mistake: **not booking museum tickets in advance.** The Uffizi and Accademia are masterpieces, yes—but the lines are brutal. On my first visit, I waited nearly two hours under a scorching June sun. After that, I learned to book online, choose off-peak hours, and always double-check holiday closures. The same goes for popular restaurants—especially those beloved by locals like Trattoria Cammillo or La Giostra. Call or reserve online a day or two ahead, and you'll be treated like family.

Florence isn't expensive if you're smart—but many fall into the trap of overpriced cafés in tourist-heavy areas. Avoid places with photo menus or hosts waving you in. Instead, walk just a few streets away from major sights. I once found a café two blocks from the Duomo where the espresso was half the price and twice as good.

And then there's **the ZTL**—a mistake that can cost hundreds of euros if you're renting a car. Florence's historic center has strict driving restrictions. Unless your hotel provides access, **do not attempt to drive into the center**. Cameras monitor every entrance, and violations result in automatic fines. Park outside and walk or use public transit.

The beauty of Florence is that she forgives your mistakes—but she rewards your care. Learn the local tempo, book smart, wander with purpose, and Florence will **open her heart to you**.

Blending In: Greetings, Style, Language, and Local Dos & Don'ts

Florence loves you more when you **act like you belong**. You don't need to be fluent in Italian, but knowing a few words goes a long way. Every morning, I started my day with a cheerful "*Buongiorno!*" to the barista, followed by "*Un caffè, per favore.*" The smile I received in return was instant and genuine. Learn how to greet shopkeepers when you enter ("*Salve*" or "*Buonasera*") and always say goodbye ("*Arrivederci*"). Italians value warmth and formality. You don't shout across a store, and you don't leave without a farewell.

Style matters, too. Florence is the birthplace of fashion, and even casual wear is elevated. Leave the gym clothes and cargo shorts at home. Think clean lines, good shoes, and neutral palettes. I noticed that even grandmothers wore scarves with effortless elegance. Dressing well isn't vanity—it's **respect**. When I wore a linen button-down and loafers, I was greeted with open arms. When I wore sneakers and a backpack, I was asked if I was lost.

Florentines also appreciate **awareness of space**. Don't block sidewalks with maps. Don't shout in churches. Speak softly in restaurants. Watch how locals move—gracefully, efficiently—and follow their lead. In markets, touch fruit only after asking. In cafés, stand at the bar for coffee unless you want to pay a table surcharge. And if someone offers help too eagerly near a major site, be cautious—it may be a scam.

One local told me, "You don't need to impress us. Just care." That stayed with me. I began to move through the city not as a guest, but as a student of its rhythms. I walked with purpose. I made eye contact. I ordered in Italian when I could, even if I stumbled. And slowly, Florence began to treat me not as a visitor, but as **someone who belonged**.

Florence will meet you where you are—but she shines brightest when you **show up with care, curiosity, and a willingness to learn**. In return, she'll teach you how to move more slowly, greet more kindly, and dress like you were always meant to be here.

Chapter 18
Emergency Numbers and Useful Contacts

I always tell people that the most beautiful trips are not only about where you wander, but how prepared you are for the unexpected. Florence, with all its art, elegance, and rhythm, can sweep you into its charm so completely that you forget the basics—how to get help if you need it, who to call, where to turn when you've lost something or someone. I learned early on that knowing these details doesn't diminish spontaneity—it enhances it. Because there's nothing more empowering than walking through a new city knowing you can handle anything. I carried a list in my notebook, dog-eared and smudged by espresso rings, of all the numbers and addresses that might just save a day or make a night easier. Let me walk you through the essentials—the lifelines of Florence when beauty meets reality.

Emergency Services: Police (112), Ambulance (118), Fire (115)

One crisp October morning, I witnessed a cyclist fall in Piazza della Repubblica. Nothing dramatic—just a sharp corner and a loose cobblestone—but it reminded me that emergencies don't send invitations. Thankfully, someone nearby dialed **112**, the **general EU emergency number**, and within minutes a local police car arrived.

In Florence, **112** connects you to police (*Carabinieri*), fire (*Vigili del Fuoco*), and ambulance (*Pronto Soccorso*) depending on the nature of the call. You'll be rerouted to the right branch—**118 for medical emergencies, 115 for fire**, and **113 (Polizia di Stato)** if you specifically need the national police service. If you're calling from a mobile and unsure who to contact, just remember **112**—they'll guide you through.

Ambulance services are fast and professional. I once had to take a friend who fainted in the summer heat to the **Ospedale Santa Maria Nuova**, and the emergency crew was efficient, kind, and English-speaking. They gave clear instructions, helped us navigate hospital protocols, and didn't expect cash upfront, though we carried our **EHIC/insurance cards** just in case.

If you feel unsafe in any neighborhood or suspect petty theft or worse, local **Carabinieri stations** (Arma dei Carabinieri) are scattered across the city and easy to access, especially in central Florence. I had a near-encounter with a bag-snatcher near Santa Maria Novella Station once and felt thankful I knew where to go. Their officers are approachable, and many speak basic English.

Safety starts with knowing you have someone to call. Write the numbers down, keep them offline, and remember: even in the city of Renaissance calm, life can surprise you.

24-Hour Pharmacies, Hospitals, and Late-Night Help

One summer night, after too much wine and a new blister from walking all day, I found myself limping through Via Roma in search of a pharmacy. That's when I discovered the beauty of **farmacie di turno**—pharmacies that rotate overnight and weekend duty in Florence. You'll find a green illuminated cross above any open pharmacy, and if one's closed, its door will usually list the nearest on-duty alternative. I ended up at **Farmacia Comunale 1** near Santa Maria Novella, open 24/7, with a warm pharmacist who offered me blister plasters, aloe, and sympathy. They speak enough English to help with travel illness, stomach bugs, jet lag, and minor allergic reactions.

If you need **medical assistance beyond the pharmacy**, Florence has reliable hospitals. The two primary public options are:

- **Ospedale Santa Maria Nuova** (Piazza Santa Maria Nuova, near the Duomo): the oldest functioning hospital in Florence, offering emergency services and urgent care. Its emergency department is well-known and used to handling tourist cases.
- **Ospedale Careggi**: larger and more specialized, located in the north of Florence, reachable by

tram. Great for more serious or specialist treatment.

There are also **private clinics**, such as **Centro Medico Misericordia** or **English-speaking general practitioners** who offer hotel visits. I once had to call a local doctor after waking up with a high fever. Within an hour, she was at my guesthouse with medicine, a gentle smile, and solid advice.

In any medical situation, keep your **passport**, **travel insurance**, and **EU health card (EHIC or GHIC)** ready. It makes paperwork easier, and in most cases, tourists won't pay upfront unless at private clinics. Always ask for a receipt—it's essential for insurance claims.

The entrance of Ospedale Santa Maria Nuova

Florence may cradle you in beauty, but when things go wrong, she's equipped to handle your pain with professionalism, quiet compassion, and just enough espresso to get you back on your feet.

Lost Items, Embassy Contacts, SIM Cards, and Tourist Information Centers

The only thing I ever lost in Florence was a scarf—twice. The first time, I left it on a café chair and recovered it ten minutes later. The second time, I wasn't so lucky. But for anything more important—passports, phones, credit cards—you'll want to know where to turn. Start with the **local police station** (*Questura*) on **Via Zara, 2**, where you can file a **"denuncia" (loss or theft report)**. I had to help a fellow traveler once whose phone was stolen on the tram. The police were efficient, gave us a copy of the report within the hour, and even called the embassy on her behalf.

Embassies and consulates in Florence or nearby Rome can assist with lost documents. The **U.S. Consulate** is in Florence at **Lungarno Vespucci 38**, while the **UK**, **Canada**, **Australia**, and **EU nations** also offer consular support either locally or from Rome. Always carry **copies of your passport**, either digital or printed, and store them separately from the original.

For minor issues or general travel help, Florence has **tourist information centers** that are surprisingly useful. My favorite is the **"Firenze Welcome" office at Piazza Stazione**—right inside the main train station. They offer maps, tips, language support, and can call a cab or connect you to emergency services in English. I stopped there once to locate a missing museum voucher and ended up chatting with a kind staff member who offered me lunch suggestions in the Oltrarno.

Now, let's talk about **SIM cards and staying connected**. You'll find plenty of shops offering **TIM**, **Vodafone**, and **WindTre** SIMs around Via Nazionale and Piazza della Repubblica. I recommend bringing your passport and choosing a prepaid plan with data—most start at €10-15. Having local data made it easy to navigate, use Google Translate, or call for help without relying on patchy Wi-Fi. I remember being lost near Piazzale Michelangelo at night and simply opening my phone to reroute myself with calm confidence.

And if you're someone who prefers not to worry about logistics, Florence offers **emergency translation services**, **taxi call booths**, and even **medical interpreting** in major hospitals. All of this is easier to access if you keep a small folder with key documents and contacts—digital and physical.

The scene should feel helpful, warm, and organized.

Losing things, feeling unwell, or needing guidance doesn't have to ruin your trip. Florence understands the delicate balance between awe and anxiety, and she's built an infrastructure that **wraps you in reassurance**. Florence, with its blend of timeless art, rich history, and vibrant culture, is a destination that lingers in your heart long after you leave. It's a place where every step brings you closer to masterpieces, where centuries-old traditions coexist with modern-day life, and where the beauty of the past continues to inspire the present.

As you reflect on your time in this magnificent city, let the memories of its stunning architecture, world-class museums, and charming streets stay with you, ready to call you back whenever you seek a glimpse of Italy's soul. Whether you came for art, history, or simply the Italian way of life, Florence offers something for everyone.

Thank you for allowing this guide to accompany you on your adventure. We hope it has helped you uncover the magic of Florence and inspired you to explore every corner of this extraordinary city. Until next time, take with you not only souvenirs, but the lasting impressions of a place that will always feel like home.

Printed in Dunstable, United Kingdom